Social Climber /so-shul cli-mur/ n:

A girl who is always working to achieve more, who improves herself each day. Call her a rising star, an up-and-coming It Girl, a fashion-forward thinker, she is nevertheless a hard worker who charms the masses and projects a unique image. If a Social Climber is aiming to improve, she also aims to be original. See also YOU, my darling reader.

Other Simon Pulse nonfiction books you might enjoy

In Their Shoes
By Deborah Reber

Doing It Right
By Bronwen Pardes

THE SOCIAL CLIMBER'S GUIDE TO HIGH SCHOOL

BY **robyn schneider**

ILLUSTRATED BY **kerrie hess**

Simon Pulse

NEW YORK   LONDON   TORONTO   SYDNEY

SIMON PULSE

An imprint of Simon & Schuster Children's Publishing Division

1230 Avenue of the Americas, New York, NY 10020

Copyright © 2007 by Robyn Schneider

Illustrations copyright © 2007 by Kerrie Hess

All rights reserved, including the right of reproduction in whole

or in part in any form.

SIMON PULSE and colophon are registered trademarks of

Simon & Schuster, Inc.

The text of this book was set in Fairfield.

Manufactured in the United States of America

First Simon Pulse edition June 2007

2 4 6 8 10 9 7 5 3

Library of Congress Control Number 2007921688

ISBN-13: 978-1-4169-3427-1

ISBN-10: 1-4169-3427-8

To Melodye Shore, for inspiration and friendship.
You're the woman I want to be when I grow up.

Infinite thank-yous to:

The A-list at Simon Pulse: My amazing and adorable editor, Michelle Nagler, and her charming, sharp assistant, Caroline Abbey. Ladies, your hilarious and heartfelt edits actually made me laugh out loud. It's been a joy working with you both! Susan Schulman, for believing in this book when it was nothing but a title. Kerrie Hess, my fabulous illustrator. The girls at Emma Willard School GirlSummer, for many things, but most notably for not making fun of me when our bus broke down by the side of the road one night, and the only light came from my laptop screen as I typed feverishly and muttered about my deadline. Leo Treysman, for being patient while I finished my edits, and for actually helping with them—it's not every teen nonfiction title that has its own medical consult. And last but certainly not least, Mom and Dad, for putting up with me when I was a teenager.

CONTENTS

The difference between school and life? In school, you're taught a lesson and then given a test. In life, you're given a test that teaches you a lesson.

—Tom Bodett

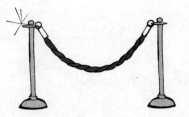

Introduction

We both know that high school isn't like the opening credits of a teen movie, with grungy guys tossing a Frisbee on the front lawn before homeroom and jocks standing around in letter jackets. Because, honestly, no one is awake enough at 8 a.m. to play sports, and if the varsity cuties are worth a second glance, they should have a better sense of style than to wear those hideous jackets on non-game days.

And what about the trio of mean girls in matching skirts, and geek girls who are transformed into hotties once they take off their glasses and pluck their unibrows? Yeah, I bet your parents believe in stuff like that too. But sweetie, you and I know better.

High school these days isn't some cheesy chick flick with a pop ballad sound track. It's a scandalous online gossip column serenaded by Fall Out Boy on an iPod. So what if you weren't invited to last night's hot party—you read about it on someone's blog and can pretend you were there if someone asks.

Instead of making time to sort your laundry, you sort your AIM Buddy List. And rather than buying a poofy-skirted prom dress and dyeing a pair of pumps to match, it's all about finding the hottest vintage designer dress and glam thrift-shop baubles to match.

If you've ever shown someone a private text message, printed out an AIM conversation, taken a secret camera phone pic of your crush, created a blog, spent the day thrifting with your girlfriends, listened to a song on a cute guy's iPod, planned an outfit the night before school, owned a wallet worth more than its contents, judged a girl by the brand of her jeans, crushed on a guy only to find him less than desirable once you caught his eye, handwritten a sideways happy face, or lied about your age to a college hottie, then you are exactly the type of girl who needs *The Social Climber's Guide to High School*. Everyone else can read *Puberty Power! Loving Your Body and Loving*

Your Soul, for all I care. And no, that isn't really the name of a book (I hope).

While other girls read patronizing self-help books in a desperate attempt to understand why they're made fun of (um, a clue? It's because they're reading patronizing self-help books), I'm going to give you some pointers on how to be even more fabulous than you already are.

Being a social climber is nothing to be ashamed of. It's not like having to ask the gym teacher for a maxi pad, or being told that your fly has been down since second period. If you're going to social climb, darling, own it! Of course, it helps if you own this book, because if I want to social climb, I'll need that new Marc Jacobs handbag, and every dollar counts. . . .

Seriously, whether you're the most popular girl in your school or B+ list on an amazing-hair day, there is stuff in this book that no adult would ever tell you (and FYI, I'm a college student, not some creepy child psychologist). After reading *The Social Climber's Guide to High School*, you'll know how to blog your way to infamy, flirt with older boys, buy designer clothes for the price of a Starbucks binge, deal with bitchy classmates, be smart in class without seeming like a know-it-all, confront problems confidently, and be your own PR person.

Now it's time to step behind the velvet rope of high school popularity. I'll see you in the VIP room, darling!

The Social Climber's Guide
to High School

The freshmen bring

a little [knowledge] in and

the seniors take none out,

so it accumulates

through the years.

—A. Lawrence Lowell

1

Social Scene It and Done That

A field guide to the fabulous halls of high school, from the A-list to the C-list

Wanna-B-Listers

Achieving campus celebrity isn't the hardest thing to do. Anyone who shows up to school in a Victorian lace gown, shaves their head, wears stilettos to P.E. for the mile run, or gets up on a lunch table and sings "Like a Virgin" is bound to be remembered. The trick is to achieve celebrity along with envy. People shouldn't just know your name: "Oh yeah, isn't that the girl who wet her pants at the pep rally?" They should want to be you: "God, she always has the coolest clothes. I just want to raid her closet, don't you?" But in order for people to know who *you* are, you need to know who *they* are, which means it's helpful to know the breakdown of the high school social scene.

Every school is different. Private schools don't have cheerleaders; public schools mostly do, unless they're magnet schools, in which case they have Westinghouse Science Scholars or summer stock actresses.

However, when you put a bunch of teenagers together in a school setting, they tend to group together. Imagine walking into Bloomingdale's and finding that men's ties are jammed onto racks with maternity tops, kiddie underroos, and designer denim. What? Exactly. If similar things weren't put together in groups of clothing racks, you'd spend hours trying to find the halter tops.

High school follows the same pattern. Just like a department store, similar types of people group together. It's easier to find students who want to star in your humorous short film if everyone at a certain lunch table is part of the theater crowd, and it's simpler to spy on your crush if he sits at the same table with his (rock) band members every day.

Although every school, like every department store, is different, there are always going to be staples—the universal cliques. These are a few:

THE IT GIRL AND THE SOCIALITES

Typically, the It Girl is the most talked about girl in school. She always has a crushworthy boyfriend, never comes to class in sweatpants and a ponytail, wears designer lip gloss and gorgeous clothes, and changes the atmosphere in a room when she walks in. Maybe she has famous parents, or lives in a huge mansion or exclusive Park Avenue apartment. Perhaps her older brother was the coolest guy in school a few years ago, or she modeled in a Lacoste ad. This girl is used to being the center of attention, the top of the guest list, the most desired, and the most envied. And, just like Barbie, she comes with accessories—Socialites.

The Socialite is the girl who flocks around the It Girl, imitating her sense of style and agreeing with her pronouncements of what is cool and what sucks. She is pretty and fashionable, a member of a mother-daughter charity league, always has a date to the dance, and has insider knowledge of the best gossip. If the It Girl disappeared, she would be replaced by one of the Socialites.

The It Girl:
* A short skirt to show off her year-round tan
* Fashionable designer shoes with an impractical heel that even look like they hurt
* Chanel sunglasses as a headband
* A status handbag that is obviously not a knockoff
* A conservative blouse that hugs curves

Chanel sunglasses as a headband

Mascara and eye makeup with no smudges

Heirloom rings and necklace, or jewelry from her boyfriend, complemented by cheap, trendy earrings

Lip gloss that her friends would never ask her to share

Hair down and long

A conservative blouse that hugs curves

Textbook and single binder for all classes, hugged to chest

A status handbag that is obviously not a knockoff

A short skirt to show off her year-round tan

THE IT GIRL

Fashionable designer shoes with an impractical heel that even look like they hurt

* Heirloom rings and necklace, or jewelry from her boyfriend, complemented by cheap, trendy earrings
* Hair down and long
* Mascara and eye makeup with no smudges
* Lip gloss that her friends would never ask her to share
* Textbook and single binder for all classes, hugged to chest

The Socialite:
* A short skirt to show off year-round tan
* Matching designer shoes that they bought together
* Hair down and noticeably highlighted
* A trendy designer handbag
* A tight, revealing shirt
* Cell phone glued to her ear
* Jewelry that is coordinated to match her outfit
* A manicure that matches her lip gloss
* A binder with photos on it
* Chewing gum she borrowed off a cute guy in second period

THE 2400 CLUB

The 2400s are the AP achievers who are bent on going to Harvard, Yale, or Columbia. They dress well, have study groups that turn into crazy parties, drive decent cars (hey, they can afford Ivy League tuition), and get together for burgers after SAT prep class. The 2400s are so serious about their grades, extracurriculars, and test scores that they don't have time to mingle with non-2400s. Lunchtime is often spent quizzing one another or at a meeting of the National Honor Society (naturally, they're officers). A 2400 exists outside of the natural order of high school cliques. She may choose to hang out with the other members of the varsity track team or not. 2400s are not nerds. They exclude the nerds in their AP classes. Like I said, they exist in their own microcosm (and they all know what that word means).

The 2400 Girl:
   * Designer jeans
   * A tight Abercrombie & Fitch button-down with a tank top peeking out underneath
   * Flip-flops
   * A heavy leather messenger bag
   * A fun watch to keep track of time during an exam

Lip gloss and mascara

Hair long and straight in a high ponytail to stay out of her face while taking notes

Cheap, fun earrings similar to the It Girl's

A tight Abercrombie & Fitch button-down with a tank top peeking out underneath

A fun watch to keep track of time during an exam

A heavy leather messenger bag

Designer jeans

THE 2400 GIRL

Flip-flops

* Hair long and straight in a high ponytail to stay out of her face while taking notes
* Lip gloss and mascara
* Cheap, fun earrings similar to the It Girl's

The 2400 Boy:
* Designer jeans
* A T-shirt bought while touring an Ivy League college
* Beat-up leather flip-flops
* Hair is shaggy and needs to be cut
* No facial hair
* North Face backpack stuffed with textbooks
* Oversize leather wristwatch, to keep track of time while taking a test
* Mechanical pencil in back pocket of jeans

THE PLAY PEOPLE

The Play People rule the Drama Club, star in the school plays, have been to summer stock theaters, and love being on the stage. They watch reruns of *Whose Line Is It Anyway?*, quote Monty Python, spend entire days talking in faux English accents for no reason, wear T-shirts with quirky sayings on them, and listen to showtunes and 80s rock. The Play People are always laughing and joking. They are both alternative and hipster, straight and gay. They have a reigning king and queen of their clique, the male and female leads of the school plays, who have usually done some "professional" acting. The stage crew and orchestra pit for the plays are not included in the Play People.

The Play Person Boy:
* Short and skinny, but that's okay because screen actors are never that tall.
* Beat-up T-shirt from a summer theater program
* Jeans with a cartoon character key chain hanging from side pocket
* Messenger bag covered in Hot Topic buttons
* Ironically bright-colored Converse All-Stars with grungy socks
* Hair is messy and sticks up in the front; sideburns are noticeable

The Play Person Girl:
* Usually has red-dyed, shoulder-length hair
* Wears a T-shirt from her favorite Broadway show, *Rent*, which she has seen five times
* Tight jeans, to compensate for T-shirt

11

Hair is messy and sticks up in the front; sideburns are noticeable

Short and skinny, but that's okay because screen actors are never that tall

Beat-up T-shirt from a summer theater program

Messenger bag covered in Hot Topic buttons

THE PLAY PERSON BOY

Jeans with a cartoon character key chain hanging from side pocket

Ironically bright-colored Converse All-Stars with grungy socks

* Slip-on checkered Vans sneakers without socks
* Chipped self-done manicure
* Messenger bag covered in Hot Topic pins that looks like it belongs to a guy
* Carries her cell phone in her back pocket in case she gets an important phone call from a casting director

THE JOCULARS

Students on sports teams see one another every day at practice and have been together all summer for training clinics. They stick together, and they're stuck together. If two girls have a falling-out over a guy, they still have to win Friday's volleyball game, and that means teamwork. The boys who play sports are generally hot (and, um, have rippling muscles) and come with a built-in group of friends for you to hang out with, should you two start going out. Girls on sports teams are usually cute, fit, and friendly. They wear their uniforms or warm-ups on game days. They have victory parties with ice cream and pizza when they win a game. Often, Joculars are also on student government. Male and female versions of the same sport create co-ed cliques. The boys and girls tennis teams typically mix together, and unfortunately the stereotype of cheerleaders and football/basketball players is also true at public schools. What is so distinct about the Joculars is that they are one large group made up of lots of little cliques: The Varsity baseball team certainly doesn't hang out with the Frosh-sophs.

The Jocular Guy:
* Polo shirt that is too tight and shows off muscles (popped collar optional)
* A warm-up jacket for his sport with his last name embroidered on the front left breast
* Baggy jeans with a rope key chain with the name of his sport printed on it dangling from a front pocket
* Dirty Adidas sneakers
* Too much hair gel shows his scalp
* Deep tan
* Light bag with an outside mesh pocket containing a Gatorade

The Jocular Girl:
* Long hair in a ponytail tied with ribbons in the school colors

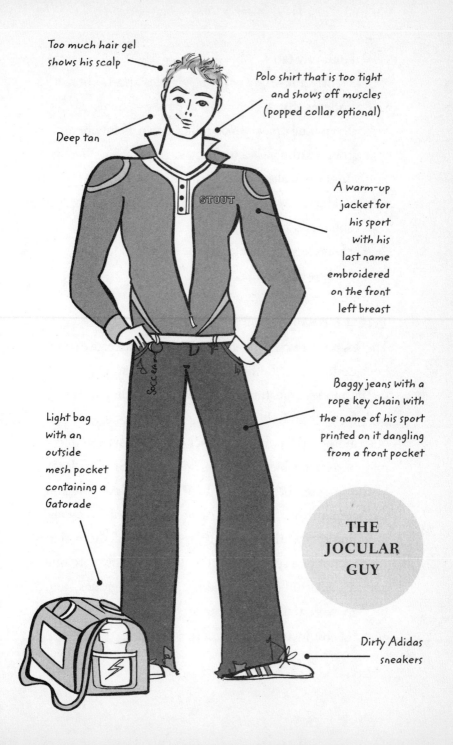

Too much hair gel shows his scalp

Polo shirt that is too tight and shows off muscles (popped collar optional)

Deep tan

STOUT

A warm-up jacket for his sport with his last name embroidered on the front left breast

Baggy jeans with a rope key chain with the name of his sport printed on it dangling from a front pocket

Light bag with an outside mesh pocket containing a Gatorade

THE JOCULAR GUY

Dirty Adidas sneakers

* Naturally tan
* Tight tank top with a visible sports bra underneath
* Navy blue track pants rolled down below her belly button
* Adidas sneakers with clean tube socks
* Backpack with a fitness bar and a vitamin-enhanced water
* Delicate silver necklace she'll have to take off for sports practice

THE J.CREW

The J.Crew are the collar-popping, seersucker-wearing, Lacoste-loving, L.L. Bean–toting preppies. They have family money, vacation on the Vineyard, play lacrosse, rugby, crew, or field hockey, and love to party—with one another. At public high schools, J.Crew members may have been kicked out of one of the St. Grotlesex boarding schools, or aspire to move to New England the moment they graduate. At private schools, they are ubiquitous, and there are often so many of them that there is not one specific J.Crew. They typically date one another, are unfailingly polite, earn good grades, and overlap with the 2400s (except they party more) and some of the Joculars (the preppy sports).

Hair is long, straight, and dark brown

Lip gloss from a pot and brown mascara

A polo shirt with the collar popped and starting to fray

A gold heirloom ring and pearl earrings

An L.L. Bean monogrammed tote bag or Vera Bradley monogramed tote bag

A jean-skirt with a fraying hem and sand in the pockets from Martha's Vineyard

j.c.g.

Espadrilles—or, if she can't be bothered to lace them up, J.Crew grosgrain flip-flops

THE J.CREW GIRL

The J.Crew Guy:
* Lacoste polo shirt with the collar popped
* Khakis from Brooks Brothers with already fraying cuffs
* J.Crew grosgrain belt with repeating pattern
* Beat-up deck shoes without socks
* Hair is shaggy and hits his collar
* An expensive watch that was a Christmas present from his father
* North Face backpack containing a ratty hooded sweatshirt from his prep school, sports team, or preppy vacation spot such as Nantucket

The J.Crew Girl:
* Hair is long, straight, and dark brown
* A polo shirt with the collar popped and starting to fray
* A jean-skirt with a fraying hem and sand in the pockets from Martha's Vineyard
* Espadrilles—or, if she can't be bothered to lace them up, J.Crew grosgrain flip-flops
* A gold heirloom ring and pearl earrings
* Lip gloss from a pot and brown mascara
* An L.L. Bean monogrammed tote bag or Vera Bradley monogramed tote bag

THE iPODS

The iPods are guys who are just as cool as the best of the Play People, Joculars, and J.Crew, but are also TDH: tall, dark, and HOTT! They wear beat-up Levi's, band T-shirts, leather jackets, black rocker-framed glasses, designer sneakers or black Converse All-Stars, and constantly listen to their iPods. These guys are usually in the process of forming a band, are heavy into the indie music scene, or are members of a local indie band. They pen song lyrics and depressing poems and take too many digital photos. They have Apple computers and shop at Urban Outfitters and smirk while they talk to you, as though they find everything hilarious. They play guitar and either love or hate The Strokes; their hair is too long and their backpacks are covered in Rolling Stones and Pink Floyd patches. These guys are the cool alternatives, the hot guys who are anti-establishment, anti–school spirit, read Vonnegut and Kerouac, and do everything *ironically*. Their groups are small, usually just three or four guys, and rarely have any female members. For some reason, they despise the J.Crew.

The iPod Guy:
* Beat-up, dirty Levi's
* A band T-shirt for an obscure, indie, or 80s rock group

Black plastic rocker-framed rectangular glasses

An iPod clipped to his front pocket, original Apple earbuds in his ears

A band T-shirt for an obscure, indie, or 80s rock group

Hair is long and floppy with sideburns and long bangs

A leather jacket, 80s style, bought in a thrift store

A beat-up old backpack covered in band patches

A guitar pick, Fender medium-thick, in his back pocket, that's gone through the wash a couple times

Beat-up, dirty Levi's

THE iPOD GUY

Black Converse All-Stars

* A leather jacket, 80s style, bought in a thrift store
* Black Converse All-Stars
* Black plastic rocker-framed rectangular glasses
* A beat-up old backpack covered in band patches
* An iPod clipped to his front pocket, original Apple earbuds in his ears
* A guitar pick, Fender medium-thick, in his back pocket, that's gone through the wash a couple times
* Hair is long and floppy with sideburns and long bangs

THE INDIES

The Indies are often on the verge of getting kicked out and having to find some alternate form of education. They dye their hair and have piercings. They are goth, emo, punk, retro, or wannabe iPods who aren't cute or cool enough. They have constant detention, are usually failing a class or two, keep depressing blogs, shop at Hot Topic, and listen to angry music. Often, they have dropped out of other cliques: a Play Person gone goth, a 2400 who started toking up. The Indies are usually a coed clique, both upperclassmen and lowerclassmen. They ditch pep rallies and don't attend the homecoming dance. They typically date one another, or date Indies from other schools whom they met on MySpace. The big difference between the iPods and the Indies is that the iPods are sarcastic, while the Indies are angry.

The Indie Guy:
* Dyed black hair
* Pierced ears with small plugs
* Black T-shirt from Hot Topic
* Dickies work pants
* Checkered slip-on Vans doodled over with ballpoint pen
* A messenger bag drawn on with Wite-Out and covered with safety pins
* Linked-together black plastic bangle bracelets on each wrist
* Wallet in back pocket and attached to a belt loop by a metal chain

The Indie Girl:
* Dyed black hair with blond streaks and short bangs
* Metal nose stud; ears are pierced all the way up in a spiral
* 50s-style jeans with a cuff

Thick makeup including bright
red lipstick and nail polish

Metal nose stud;
ears are pierced
all the way up in a
spiral

Dyed black hair
with blond streaks
and short bangs

A vintage 50s-
style polka-dot
blouse

Disney-character
lunch box as a purse

Plastic bangle
bracelets up
one arm

50s-style jeans
with a cuff

Scuffed vintage 80s
pumps from a thrift
store

THE
INDIE
GIRL

* A vintage 50s-style polka-dot blouse
* Scuffed vintage 80s pumps from a thrift store
* Disney-character lunch box as a purse
* Thick makeup including bright red lipstick and nail polish
* Plastic bangle bracelets up one arm

THE CONS

The Cons are the typically geeky guys and girls who are into different fandoms. They read fantasy and science fiction novels, build their own websites, get good grades, sketch anime characters, and have been to at least one Con—that's a convention, like for anime or fantasy or sci-fi or comics. Even though they are a coed clique, they don't date one another, and are usually immature and don't care about fashion. They can be quiet girls who watch *Sailor Moon*, pudgy freshman boys who read Manga sitting on the floor of the Barnes & Noble, or online gamers. They overlap with different social activities such as the marching band or French Club, and are not part of the 2400s even though they take classes together and are both cliques looking to get into top-tier colleges. They sometimes associate with or turn into Indies.

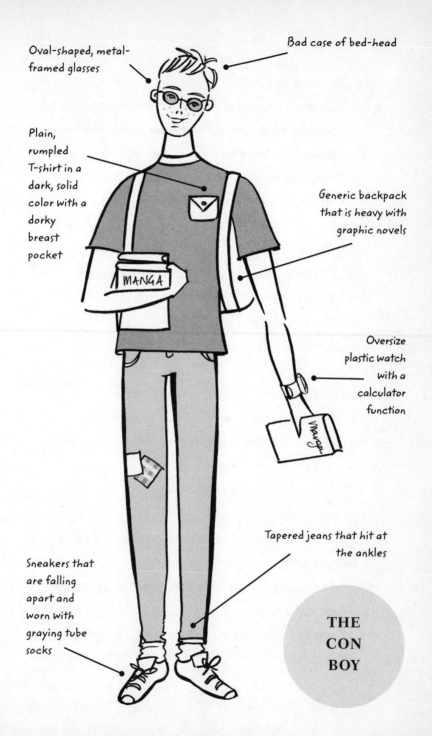

Oval-shaped, metal-framed glasses

Bad case of bed-head

Plain, rumpled T-shirt in a dark, solid color with a dorky breast pocket

MANGA

Generic backpack that is heavy with graphic novels

Oversize plastic watch with a calculator function

Tapered jeans that hit at the ankles

Sneakers that are falling apart and worn with graying tube socks

THE CON BOY

The Con Boy:
* Tapered jeans that hit at the ankles
* Sneakers that are falling apart and worn with graying tube socks
* Plain, rumpled T-shirt in a dark, solid color with a dorky breast pocket
* Generic backpack that is heavy with graphic novels
* Glasses are oval-shaped and metal-framed
* Sporting a bad case of bed-head
* Oversized plastic watch with a calculator function

The Con Girl:
* Hair in a low ponytail or down (in which case it is extremely long, medium brown, and wavy)
* Jeans that have an unfashionable high rise and are slightly too short
* Black unisex T-shirt, advertising favorite anime program
* Backpack covered in key chains of anime characters
* Cross-trainer shoes picked out by parents
* No makeup

There are other cliques besides the Socialites, 2400s, J.Crew, Play People, Joculars, iPods, Cons, and Indies, but I think that the other cliques are combinations of these eight. The Debate Team, for example, is a mix of the 2400s, the Cons, and the J.Crew. Student Government is a blend of the J.Crew, the Joculars, and the 2400s.

Hot (Student) Body

Instead of picturing each group of students separately, it helps to picture them as part of a larger scene. If high school is an exclusive nightclub, only the beautiful A-list people are in the VIP room—but it doesn't matter. Sometimes being under the constant paparazzi and tabloid scrutiny of the VIP room is too much pressure, and it's better to just hang out on the dance floor with everyone else on the B-list. Or maybe the anticipation of getting accepted by the bouncer is your thing, leaving you waiting in line and horsing around with the rest of the C-list.

There are positives and negatives to being a member of each social strata:

THE PERKS OF BEING AN A-, B-, OR C-LISTER

	A-LIST ARISTOCRAT	B-LIST BABE	C-LIST CHIC
PROS	• Invites to the best parties • An all-access pass to the hottest guys • Insta-celebrity on campus • An entourage of beautiful people • A full-to-bursting social calendar	• Semi-access to the best parties • The possibility of dating the coolest guys • Being quasi-known on campus • Having friends with the same interests as you (besides Chanel lip gloss) • A balanced social and study calendar	• Zero peer pressure to attend parties • Dating friends you've known for a while • Being able to show up to class in sweatpants without being gossiped about • Having time to do what you want
CONS	• Less time to do work because you're always being social • Hot self-centered jerks you have to date to maintain your image • Constant scrutiny and judgment—it seems like everyone hates you/is afraid of you • Being part of someone else's entourage • No time to yourself	• Hearing about a party you weren't invited to and being hurt because you weren't invited • Having A-list girls snag the best guys • Being gossiped about when you thought you were under the radar • Friends who are too competitive • Worrying about what to do over the weekend	• Never knowing weekend gossip because you weren't where the scandal happened • Dating and getting dumped by some loser • Feeling socially invisible • Having friends who suddenly get too cool to hang with you • Having nowhere to go on the weekend

SOCIAL CHUTES AND LADDERS:
WAYS TO SOCIAL CLIMB AND SOCIAL STUMBLE

LADDERS

C-LIST TO B-LIST	B-LIST TO A-LIST
• Getting your braces removed	• Getting a nose job (well, it's true)
• Discovering tweezers	• Developing an awesome sense of style/starting a fashion craze
• Ditching an out-of-necessity lunch group that only drags you down	• Getting "discovered" by a non-scamming talent scout/modeling agency and consequently landing airtime on a hot teen drama (even being an extra counts!)
• Dressing stylishly (but NOT imitating the It Girl—that would be a poseur move)	
• Joining and making a good impression on a socially acceptable club or team	• Being elected to a high student government position, team captain of a prestige sport, or president of an elite group
• Getting an awesome car for your sixteenth birthday	
• Throwing an incredible party (but if no one shows or no one knows you hosted it, this could backfire)	• Getting an awesome car for your sixteenth birthday
• Having a status-boyfriend (see Chapter 2)	• Throwing an incredible party (but if your friends take credit, they could become A-list and ditch you)
	• Having a status-boyfriend (see Chapter 2)

CHUTES

A-LIST TO B-LIST	B-LIST TO C-LIST
• Not being invited to parties anymore, and thus not being included in your friends' weekend plans	• Not being invited to the hottest parties, and then missing the key gossip and having to be filled in with the rest of the school
• Having a social-climbing so-called friend ditch you, leaving you groupless or with significantly less popular friends	• Getting dumped publicly, or by a status-boyfriend
• Dating a loser, or getting dumped publicly in a brutal fashion	• Being the object of scandalous gossip
• Being the object of slanderous gossip/nasty rumors	• The arrival of a new student who takes your role as one of the It Girl's social satellites
• The arrival of a new student who takes over your role in your clique, placing you in a subordinate satellite position, gravitating around someone else's shining star	• Being ostracized by the It Girl
• Being ostracized by your clique	• Throwing a bad party
• Throwing a dorky party (e.g., parent chaperones, Spice Girls music)	• Losing a public election to someone noticeably less popular
• Dropping out of a defining social activity (e.g., quitting a varsity sport)	• Crashing your car (i.e., no longer having wheels, which really sucks if you usually drove people around, but could get you major sympathy if you wind up in the hospital)
• Dropping out of the advanced classes (disassociating with the 2400s)	• And the obvious: getting knocked up, doing drugs, getting arrested for shoplifting
• Losing car privileges and thus having to scramble for a ride if you want to go anywhere	
• And the obvious: getting knocked up, doing drugs, getting arrested for shoplifting	

In order to social climb, you must constantly strive to associate with people who have high social status, people who are interesting, and people who appreciate you. It's a delicate balance and, depending on your strengths and weaknesses, unique to each social climber.

Frenemies of the State

We've been talking about cliques, but what about friends— i.e., the people who make up these groups? Groups all have the same dynamic: A Fendi bag carries lip gloss, a wallet, and a cell phone, just like a bag from Payless. The contents of an A-list clique aren't that different from the contents of a C-list clique.

First, there's the CEO. She runs the clique. If she says one of the members is a loser, everyone else better believe it. If she says skinny jeans are out, no way is anyone in her clique going to wear their favorite pair tomorrow. Her opinions matter, and without her, the clique wouldn't exist. She is the CEO of the group because she started it, or she dethroned the original CEO. She is friends with everyone in the group, and even though she may not be universally liked, her commands are universally respected. She has more going for her than the other members of the clique, and she keeps her power by subtly making it known that she is better than everyone else.

Next there are the Members Only. These girls are friendly with the CEO and were invited into the group by her. They are often better friends with one another than with the CEO, but they feel guilty when they hang out without her. It is their job to agree with what she says and to do what she wants. They are slightly less popular than the CEO, but all of them are at an equal popularity level. They secretly resent the CEO and plot to get rid of her, but never follow through.

Finally, there are the Straphangers. Usually there is only one of these per group. This is the girl who is not quite on the same level as everyone else. Sometimes she tries too hard and is too desperately sucking up to not only the CEO but the entire clique. No one really likes her, but how can they get rid of her if she won't take a hint? The Straphanger attaches herself to whom she sees as either the weakest or strongest member of the clique and annoys them with her clinginess. She calls too often, sends too many e-mails, is too eager to volunteer. The only good thing about having her around is getting to mock her and trash her behind her back (and sometimes to her face).

And all of these girls, the CEO, the Members Only,

and the Straphangers, are brought together and often pulled apart by the glue that holds high school together: gossip.

GOSSIP GIRLS

> If you can't say something good
> about someone, sit right here by me.
>> —Alice Roosevelt Longworth

An important part of the clique dynamic is gossip, but there is so much more to gossiping than just telling a nasty rumor.

THE 411 ON THE GOSSIP GIVER

This is the girl who has found out a juicy tidbit of gossip that is just too delicious to keep to herself. She is creating a scandal. By telling, she releases this gossip into her high school, which means that it WILL become common knowledge, and that it can be traced back to her. Maybe she is betraying a friend—or an enemy. Perhaps she has been "frenemies" (sometimes a friend, sometimes an enemy) with another girl for too long and is returning the favor of nasty gossip. Maybe she has been dumped and is telling secrets about her ex-boyfriend. Or maybe she is trying to social climb.

Spreading gossip is NEVER an appropriate way to social climb. Not because it's rude and hurtful (I'm not your mom—I don't care that you "do unto others") but because it hurts you. First of all, you have to pick whom to tell, which usually means that you'll be telling someone you want to impress—i.e., you come off as desperate for their approval. They should be desperate for *your* approval, darling. Second, you never know when gossip can backfire. If the subject of your gossip traces the rumor back to you, he or she could tear you down. Or, if someone is really hurt, they could tell their parents and you could wind up getting sent to the principal's office (which is SO embarrassing—not like I'd know).

> It isn't what they say about you, it's what they whisper.
>
> —Errol Flynn

If you insist on gossiping, here are five scenarios in which it is acceptable, and five in which it is totally verboten.

Green-Light Gossip: Go Ahead!
1. Hanging out with your girlfriends after school, once someone has already initiated the gossip session (never be the first to start gossiping).

2. If you feel your social status slipping and you need to reclaim your role as CEO of your clique by showing them that you are a privileged insider and have the information to prove it.

3. If you've just broken up with a status boyfriend and need to make it clear that he was the one unworthy of you.

4. A girl you don't like has already been torn down by juicy gossip, and you have more to add—it doesn't help, and it certainly doesn't make you a nice person, but it doesn't hurt you.

5. Celebrity gossip is always a plus, especially if it's firsthand and not ganked from the tabloids.

Red-Light Rumors: Stop!

1. Never go up to a significantly more popular girl and share gossip. This makes you come off as a Straphanger, or a wannabe who needs her approval.

2. Never share gossip over the phone. How do you know it isn't a trick and the girl your

friend is egging you on to trash isn't listening to the whole thing on three-way calling?

3. AIM. Never ever *ever* put mean things in writing, and yes, this includes e-mail and text messaging. People can save these and print them out or show them to others if you guys start fighting. Bad, bad idea.

4. Don't blog about it unless your claim to fame is having a campus-known gossip blog. Seriously, more people read your blog than you'd imagine. Maybe your *mom* reads your blog. You don't need her having a talk with you about playing nice.

5. Never gossip at school. I mean this. You don't know who could overhear. Gossip doesn't help you social climb, it just helps you maintain your social status if you're starting to slip. Never let your classmates hear you gossip. You should appear to have better things to do than discuss so-and-so's period stain on the back of her pants. I mean, aren't you more important than that? Aren't you above petty

gossip? Well, honey, none of us is above it, but we like to pretend we are—at least in front of the unimportant people.

GOSSIP MAKES THE WORLD GO ROUND

Who gossips with you will gossip of you. —Irish saying

What do you do if your well-intended arrow misses the mark and you find yourself unarmed in nasty, gossipy territory? Read on, sweetie, to find out how to turn a situation from nearly catastrophic into barely catty.

You're getting dressed after a ridiculous P.E. class where all you did was stand on the tennis courts and pretend to serve when the teacher looked your way. It sucked, you're cranky, and someone just sprayed some foul designer imposter perfume all over the locker room. Blech. Now your friend is talking to you while she brushes her hair. She's gossiping about a girl you're friends with.

". . . and then I heard her fart in the next toilet stall after she peed. I knew it was her because I looked at her shoes."

Your move, sweetie. Want some help?

Okay, you're in a public place. Don't join in the gossip session. You never know who's listening, or if the girl you're talking about is one row of lockers away. Even though you're in a pissy mood and it would feel so good to blow off some steam by engaging in a bitch-fest, don't make your friend your target. You don't social climb by losing friends. Here are some things to say in order to stop a gossip session from starting in a place where it would be inappropriate to gossip.

* "Why are you obsessed with her?"
* "I don't feel like discussing this."
* "Why are we even talking about this?"
* "Like you haven't ever done the exact same thing?"
* "And I care why?"
* "You know she's a friend of mine, so I don't know why you would tell me this."

TALKING (SH)IT GIRLS

Maybe it's something in their lip gloss, but some girls are just plain bitches. They automatically assume that they're the number one when you get together, and I don't know about you, but I've never been one to play sidekick (although Sidekick is a different matter, especially the ones with the pink Swarovski crystals). Sometimes you need to get a situation back into control by letting a girl know that if she wants a number two, she better get a pencil. Here are some sneak-attactics to get the message across:

* Tell her to meet at your house and when she gets there, continue getting ready while complaining about how late you are. Then turn to her and say, "Sweetie, my friend we're meeting is going to kill me for being this late, so we need to tell him that you showed up at my house an hour after I told you to." This puts her in the position of taking the fall for your "mistake."

* Act as though you are about to divulge a huge secret and then stop yourself and say, "No, I don't know if I can trust you with this." Make her beg.

* Introduce her to a friend of yours and forbid them beforehand from exchanging contact information. If they want to see each other again, it's either behind your back or on your terms.

Sure, it's not nice to act this way, but if you're trying to teach a brat a lesson, sometimes it's best to fight cattiness with cattiness. Just consider it holding a mirror up and giving your frenemy a glimpse of her ugly self.

Highlights at the End of the Tunnel

Some chapters end with a cliffhanger, others end with SparkNotes. But this chapter, after navigating the minefield of high school cliques and stereotypes, ends with a simple question: Which are you?

SOCIALITE, SOCIAL BUTTERFLY, OR SOCIAL CLIMBER?

If you love being granted access beyond the velvet rope, catching attention as the star of the party, or being photographed for the society pages (or at least the yearbook), you are, my dear, a social girl, and that's just fabulous. But what type of social scenerista are you?

THE SOCIALITE

The Socialite is always spotted looking gorgeous at the best house parties and school events. She loves going out simply because it's fun, and because she can't stand being alone. She is popular, of course, but beyond that, she is effortlessly stylish and constantly chased by adorable boys. Her phone's ring tone never gets a rest as everyone calls with invitations. The Socialite never sits at home on a Friday night watching TV. She is social, social, social, and her calendar pages are so full, they look like they have been injected with collagen. She is not very involved with school activities, and her only claim to fame is that she seems to do nothing besides showing up everywhere worth going and having a carefree good time.

THE SOCIAL BUTTERFLY

The Social Butterfly flutters from table to table. Everyone wants to be her friend, and there is not enough of her to go around, but she tries nonetheless. She is effortlessly like-able, constantly lusted after, and apt to be found at a trendy caf) with some gossiping girlfriends, a loud keg party that's not exactly A-list, the most exclusive party of the semester, or a late-night diner with a girl she just met at the mall and decided to spend the day with. She is beautiful and alluring, and she never settles down with one group of friends, or one activity. Sometimes she is home alone, sometimes she is at the movies. She never knows who is going to call her, or who she should call in a crisis, but there is always someone. Her life is a rotating blur of glamour and guys, but nothing feels exactly right, which is why she is still searching for the best friend, the best clique, the best scene to attach her wonderful self to.

THE SOCIAL CLIMBER

The Social Climber is a girl with a purpose. She is fashionable and fun, mysterious and talked about. No one knows exactly where she is on any given night, but no doubt it's somewhere fabulous. She may be home alone on a Friday night, but no one knows that. She is an individual, effortlessly cool, the girl the boys wish they could have. Her mission is to be even more fab than she already is. She only associates with the best and most interesting people. She never puts others down or engages in public gossip. Her boyfriend is always a jealousy-making hottie, and if she's single, it means being single is in this season. She is invited to the best parties, and if she isn't, she finds a way to go anyway, or something better to do with her time. She is sophisticated and glamorous. She may talk about art and watch foreign films, or pronounce the names of certain fashion designers with an impeccable French accent. No one can resist her charms, because she truly is a rising star, an up-and-coming It Girl. But beneath all that, she is a hard worker who projects a unique image, and always works to improve herself. After all, darling, you can never be wonderful enough.

Gift Bag #1:
Membership in the Social Climber's Club

Before embarking upon your journey up the social ladder, it's time to swear you into our little club. From now on, you are not just a social climber but a Social Climber. Repeat after me:

I believe that I am fabulous, and it is true. If I work hard enough, the velvet rope will grant me entry. If I am unique, then I am true to myself and my friends will not be false to me. I give myself the chance to let others see how wonderful I am, and in doing so, I will not betray the Sisterhood of the Social Climbers.

Now that you are a full Social Climber, here are our guidelines:

The Social Climber's Code of Conduct

1. A Social Climber is never boring. Have

you ever spoken to a girl for just a minute and thought, *She is so much more interesting than me!* The truth is, this girl may be the most interesting person on the planet, or maybe she isn't. But she knows how to spin herself to *seem* fascinating.

How to be interesting:

* Always have a highlight of your day ready to share, and if nothing happened, make one up, or talk about something interesting that happened earlier in the week. That way, when someone calls and asks you what you're up to, you have something prepared and never just mumble, "Nothing." A Social Climber is never up to "nothing."

* Find a new hobby. Is there something you've always wanted to try? Well, why haven't you done it? Look into lessons or getting a job if you have the free time, or you can teach yourself. If money is a problem, babysit to cover some of the expense and ask your parents if they're prepared to cover the rest. They'll be surprised at your initiative and maturity. Become a jewelry designer or a horse-

back rider, intern at an art gallery, join a charity league and organize a fashion show benefit, write and film a movie, learn to play the electric guitar, take French lessons, join a fencing class, or start an online zine.

* Return questions. If someone asks you what you did over the weekend, respond with a fun anecdote and then promptly ask them the question back. People love to talk about themselves, and if they asked you the question, chances are they have an answer in mind themselves.

* Believe that people are interested in what you say. I could tell you about the *Hamptons* magazine launch party I just went to, about how this one girl stole a lip gloss right out of my gift bag and then had the nerve to admit it to my face, like I owed her the lip gloss. (And, seriously, who steals swag? I mean, it's free. Just go get your own.) But if I told you this story in a quiet monotone, looking at my lap or over your shoulder, you wouldn't care. It's not a juicy tidbit unless it sounds like

one. Always speak with passion, and even if the story you are telling is a recycled one, smile and gesture as though all the jokes have just occurred to you.

2. **A Social Climber is always kind.** We've gone over the gossip no-no's already, but I want to stress that no one actually likes someone who's mean. Mean girls don't social climb—they are resented, not befriended. The girls who go out of their way to be friends with them are Straphangers who are trying to get something out of the friendship, not the kind of people you want to associate with.

Even if you are having a bad day, there is no reason to be negative. Complaining, whether about people or a specific event or just the general ickiness of high school, isn't a smart move. You should seem like you are happy all of the time (not perky-happy, which is like omigod super annoying heeheehee!!!!!!), but like you are a person who is fun to be around and has a good time. People will want to have a good time with you, and they will want to hang out with you and invite you places.

Manners matter. If you go over to someone's house, make sure to be polite to their
parents and nice to their siblings. If a girl's
kid sister thinks you are really cool, she'll let
her big sister know. Little siblings make great
fans, and they promote you. ("When is that
cool girl coming over again? I liked her. She
said she'd bring me a copy of her Death Cab
for Cutie CD.")

**3. A Social Climber will help another
Social Climber when asked.** Never make
the mistake of thinking that you are the only
Social Climber out there. And just like a girl
can have more than one best friend, a school
can have more than one Social Climber. Help
each other out, and you can only benefit. If
she succeeds and owes you, you succeed.
Extend a party invite, and good karma will see
that you get one in return.

If the girl seems to be taking more than
giving, use your discretion for when you should
stop passing out freebies. After all, you're not a
PR person for anyone but yourself.

4. A Social Climber will not associate herself with people who drag her down.
You know that girl who couldn't get a clue if it came stapled to her favorite Old Navy classic-fit sandblasted jeans? She thinks you're supercool, and, well, you are, but you won't be for long if she keeps telling everyone that you're friends. You feel sorry for her, so she sits at your lunch table and you haven't said anything about it. She got your phone number out of the school directory and she calls you every weekend asking if you want to come over and make jigsaw puzzles. She eats a stinky tuna sandwich every day and always offers you half. She has a class with you, gets there early, saves a seat and waves you over but you don't refuse. But worse than any of these things, she seems to have no opinions of her own, agreeing with whatever you say even if she's just said the opposite. She isn't someone you can talk to, and when you spend time together you don't wind up having fun.

It may hurt you a lot to tell her that you don't want to be friends, but it will hurt her more if someone else gives her the memo she's been missing and doesn't sugar coat it.

You don't need an insane enemy on a stinky tuna warpath glaring at you every time you dress out for P.E. You need to do something. Tell her the truth, that you don't think you have much in common, or that it bothers you the way she changes her opinion and doesn't seem to have any ideas of her own. Be kind, but also be firm, and make sure she understands that you're just not having fun when the two of you spend time together.

Don't let people guilt you into hanging out with them, because those people are Straphangers, hitching a ride on your express train to campus celebrity and making you feel crowded.

5. **A Social Climber was born to be talked about, but on her terms.** Spin your own gossip. If you're mindful of the way you act and the image you project, you have no one to blame but yourself if you aren't received with open arms and a million invitations to hang out next weekend. Either that, or some hater is gossiping about you. Instead of gossiping back,

confront her and figure out why she dislikes you. If you're a positive person with interesting hobbies and confidence, who doesn't mimic the exact clothing styles of girls in the top A-list clique, and hasn't been the brunt of a bad breakup, no one should be gossiping about you in a way that could actually hurt. Take a step back, a deep breath, a trip for some retail therapy, and then reconsider. Is the gossip really that harmful? If it is, figure out how it started and trace it to the root. If it doesn't seem likely to blow over in a day or two, you need to drop a few phrases into conversation, or make a fake blog post about something fabulous that will get people gossiping about you in a better way (more about this in the next chapter).

6. **A Social Climber is unique.** You will never be a blond girl in a black tank top, jean skirt, and cheap flip-flops walking through the mall with no purse and her equally generic two friends. Instead, be the girl in the cat-eye vintage reading glasses, the girl who put collectable postage stamps on a vintage Fendi bag, the girl who reads the *Wall Street Journal*

in homeroom, the girl who writes an advice column in the local paper, the girl who takes notes with a fountain pen.

Being quirky is a good thing. It gives people a reason to remember you. Pick your quirk and stick with it, and you'll never be "Wait, who?" again.

7. **A Social Climber works to improve herself.** There are tons of ways to make yourself even more awesome than you already are, and since you can never be fabulous enough, go for it. Just like famous fashion designers improve their collections each season, you should improve yourself each season, whether with a new hobby, trying to break yourself of an old habit, or a self-betterment kick to actually watch the news (or at least the first fifteen minutes).

8. **A Social Climber makes friends, not enemies.** It's easier to make enemies than friends. Sometimes it seems like teenage girls get up in the morning and decide to hate everyone who isn't in their clique. If the It Girl of a group

decides that she doesn't like someone, her friends don't like that girl either. But it is easy to make friends if you're a true Social Climber. You can slip into any situation, say something charming and interesting, compliment the person you're talking to, and return their questions, and they'll be wondering how they can hang out with you again. Focus on making people like you rather than just letting out your feelings. Complain about your nasty Spanish teacher or the fight you just had with your mom to a best friend, not to someone you're merely friendly with. You're not out to make people hate you, but sometimes they do, and then:

9. **A Social Climber makes the best of any situation.** Sometimes it happens. Girls get jealous. They think you're "pretentious" or "fake." They gossip about you and bitch to their friends. Believe me, those people aren't making themselves look any better by being haters, so don't trouble yourself.

If you're ever in a really bad situation, don't panic or act as though you are the victim. Beautiful people are never victims who run to their friends in a panic, begging for advice (and voluntarily placing themselves in a subordinate social position).

If you just showed up at a party and your ex-boyfriend is there, don't avoid him, but smile from across the room so he knows that you're there and that you're comfortable being at the same party.

Turn bad situations to your advantage by calling positive attention to yourself. Don't laugh like an idiot or ignore the problem, but ride it through and turn it into something else so your trip down the icy stairs turns into a cafeteria-tray sled run, or your melted pot of lip gloss becomes finger paint where every girl at the table has to write the name of her crush on her napkin.

10. **A Social Climber is not necessarily the most popular girl in school, but she is okay with that.** If you social climb success-fully, you'll eventually reach the top, but when you do, there's nowhere else to go. If you're the most popular girl in your school, you're no longer a social climber, and what fun is there in that? Okay, a lot, but it's like going to the

mall and giving yourself the okay to buy one semi-extravagant item. You don't know what you'll buy, so browsing is exciting. After you've found the item you want, though, going home with it is a letdown. Sure, it's gorgeous, but now you can't go shopping for a while. The first time you wear it, some of the excitement returns, but after you've worn it for a while, it's not even that wonderful anymore. Popularity is the same way. The thrill of hunting for the best, sifting through the possibilities, and making the decision of what you want and are willing to have worked to earn is the thrill of social climbing. Climbing is such fun, but once you reach the top of the social mountain, you have nothing to do except sit there and hope no one makes you climb *down* the mountain.

There are perks to being A-list, B-list, and C-list, darling. And hey, if you're really dissatisfied with where you wind up, maybe it's time to convince your parents to let you transfer schools. After all, according to Oscar Wilde, "There are only two tragedies in life: one is not getting what one wants, and the other is getting it."

Some students drink from the fountain of knowledge. Others just gargle.

—E. K. McKenzie

CHAPTER 2

Gems of Wisdom Are a Girl's Best Friend

How to be smart in a smart way

GPA-List

There's nothing wrong with focusing on the social aspect of high school as long as you don't neglect your grades. Ever heard the phrase "brains and beauty"? That's the ultimate combination. So spin the combination on your locker from social to scholastic for a moment and listen up.

There's a big difference between being smart and being nerdy. If you get an A on a science project, go you! But if you get an A on a science project that you've spent every spare moment working on since the summer and have unsuccessfully tried to patent, then honey, step away from the test tubes.

A smart girl knows when to speak up in class and what to say so that her classmates won't form a negative opinion of her. She has great study skills and finishes her homework well and quickly, leaving more time for the things she wants to do. Her parents trust her after seeing her report card and give her more freedom, including a later curfew and possibly access to a car. She makes friends in class by always pulling her weight in a group project rather than burdening others with her slack. As a senior, she's accepted no sweat to her top college and can relax for the final months of high school knowing that all those homework assignments have amounted to something.

Trust me, you don't want to peak in high school. There's nothing worse than living at home, working some dorky minimum-wage retail job, and taking three community college credits with no plans to transfer. Actually, there is something worse: doing this and watching your former classmates come home at Christmas break from their elite schools where they've been having the time of their lives. Suddenly the status quo will have shifted, and it will suck.

So take some preventative action from becoming a has-been at the age of eighteen: Embrace your inner intellectual. Whether that means knowing how to insult your sworn enemy in SAT-worthy language, learning how to sound smart in class without dominating a discussion, or faking your way through a conversation about theater, read on, and climb your way to the top of the academic A-list.

LIKE LIKE?

You know those girls in class who always say "like" and "you know" five times in every sentence? It is, like, so annoying, you know? You don't want to listen to them. In fact, I bet you tune them out. They don't sound like they're saying anything important, so you assume they aren't.

In order for people to listen to you, you need to make sure they're paying attention. So make sure you:

1. never talk over someone else.

2. say, "I'm sorry, may I finish speaking?" or, "Go ahead," if interrupted.

3. say, "I'm sorry, what were you saying?" if interrupting someone.

4. watch that you don't "um" or "uhhh" too often.

5. avoid up-talking, which is ending every sentence? Like it's a question? And you aren't sure of

what you're saying? *Très* annoying, no?

6. never whisper, even in a dorky Spanish class when you're reading the answer to a homework question. Speaking loudly (but not yelling) shows that you are confident and expect to be heard.

7. never belittle yourself when speaking in class by starting with, "I was just going to say . . ." or, "Maybe this is irrelevant, but . . ." Don't make excuses for expressing your opinions, or people won't care enough to find out what they are.

Remember, darling, every Social Climber wants to be heard. She is just too fabulous to remain silent, no matter how shy she really is.

SPEAK EASY

Now that you're not going to sit in the back of the classroom and read *Teen Vogue* inside of your textbook, it's time to figure out what you're going to say.

You definitely don't want to be the obnoxious girl who dominates the discussion, talking about the different tropes that the author posits within his rupture of the societal norms that are contained within the overarching theme of his text, but you should, um, speak up.

It's best to aim to contribute one point to the discussion each period. Now, if you absolutely suck at physics, you don't need to talk in that class every day, but you should try to contribute at least once a week in your worst subject.

Unfortunately, speaking up in school means that you need to do the homework—yes, all of it. Before you raise your hand, make sure you have something to say. You don't want to bore everyone catatonic by umming your way through a bunch of vaguely phrased garbage.

Some phrases you might find useful for discussion in an **English class** are:

* The author doesn't seem to be getting his point across effectively here because . . .

* The author is trying to teach us [this] but I wind up wondering whether . . .

* I'm curious whether there any events in the author's life that prompted his views on . . .

* One problem I see with our discussion is that we've been focusing on [this] rather than . . .

* Even though [person who spoke before me] made a really good point, I don't think this issue here is really [this] but rather . . .

* It's interesting to note the similarities between this character and the author's own experience with . . .

* The voice here is so distinct that I don't think we can focus wholly on imagery without also considering point of view.
* What struck me about this particular piece is how different it is from other works being produced at the time, such as . . .

HELPFUL WORDS FOR NON-HISTORY BUFFS

* **Echelon.** It means different levels of society. Example: The lower echelon citizens in a feudal society were the peasants.
* **Bicameral legislature.** A government with two legislative branches. Example: Because of our federal government's balance of power, our bicameral legislature functions through a series of checks and balances.
* **Suffrage.** The right to vote. Example: Elizabeth Cady Stanton and Susan B. Anthony were the founders of the American women's suffrage movement.
* **Mercantilism.** A protectionist policy where the ruling government plays a hand in the economy by encouraging exports and discouraging imports through the use of tariffs. Example: Adam Smith's theories on

laissez-faire economics ended the practice of European mercantilism.

* **Jingoism.** A pushy form of patriotism that advocates bullying other countries in order to safeguard one's own country's national interests. Example: Through much of the Victorian period, Britain held a jingoist stance toward Russia as the two empires battled for supremacy in Central Asia.

Wait, I heard . . . What I'm learning in math is not applicable in the real world. FALSE! Say there's going to be an after-Christmas sale at Urban Outfitters. All jeans are 50 percent off and an additional 10 percent off the sale price. You have a $20 gift card. How much money do you need to add to your gift card to buy that great-looking pair of low-slung, dark-rinse Diesels?

The equation: $(0.5j \times 0.9) - 20 = m$ where j = the original price of the jeans and m = how much you have to add to the gift card to buy them.

Say the jeans are $100. $[0.5(100) \times 0.9] = 45$

$45 - 20 = 25$. Solution? Add $25 to your gift card.

Smart idea: Whenever possible, make a PowerPoint presentation. It impresses teachers, is fast and easy to create, and serves as a visual during your oral report so students don't get bored.

TESTING . . . 1, 2, 3: EXAM-TAKING TIPS

* Flip through the exam before you begin to get an idea of its length.
* Divide the number of problems by the number of minutes you have to complete the exam, giving you a general idea of how long you have on each question.
* Mark easy questions and difficult questions, then skip around and complete all of the easy ones first. Next tackle the medium-difficulty questions, and finally the hardest.
* Write neatly—if the grader can't read your answer, it's wrong.
* If you finish early, double-check your answers. It seems boring, sure, but what else are you going to do with ten minutes of silent class time?

EXTRA CREDIT: REWARDS FOR DOING WELL IN SCHOOL

If you're not allowed to watch TV until your homework is finished, ask your parents to order TiVo or DVR. A DVR service (about $10 a month) or TiVo service (about $15 a month) will allow you to program shows you want to record in advance. Just explain to your parents that you would spend more time and attention on your homework if you weren't trying to finish by the time *America's Next Top Model* came on. If you could record your favorite shows, you would be able to focus more on your schoolwork without feeling like you're missing something. Offer to pick up an extra chore around the house to earn DVR or TiVo if your parents aren't just going to agree to an extra expense for no reason. This way, you'll never be left out of a conversation in school because you had to write a paper the day before and missed the first half of the show they're talking about.

TAKE ME OUT

> Heather: It's just like Hamlet said,
> "To thine own self be true."
> Cher: Hamlet didn't say that.
> Heather: I think I remember *Hamlet*
> accurately.
> Cher: Well, I remember Mel Gibson
> accurately, and he didn't say
> that. That Polonius guy did.
> —from CLUELESS

It doesn't matter if you're out with your girlfriends or a hot guy, or just having a post-class chat with your teacher, you should always know what you're talking about. If someone corrects you, they have the upper hand in the situation. And honey, since no one knows everything about everything, sometimes it's just best to fake it.

DA VINCI DECODED

Art galleries scream sophistication, but they also scream déclassé if you don't know what to say about the art. So, next time someone asks for your input on a particular piece, try one of these ten phrases:

1. There's something so enigmatic about the artist's pain.

2. This is a fabulous example of texture.

3. Notice the artist's use of balance in this area.

4. I love the sweeping lines.

5. The brush strokes are incredibly bold.

6. I love the interplay of the warm and cool colors.

7. There's something off about the composition.

8. The depth astounds me.

9. What an interesting perspective.

10. The colors are so expressive.

ROCK THE CASBAH: HOW TO PASS YOURSELF OFF AS AN INDIE ROCKER

* Dress like a scenester from the East Village: American Apparel hoodie, skinny jeans, Vans slip-ons, cheesy jewelry.

* When asked about the new album of a band you've never heard of, say, "Yeah, their old stuff is better."

* Relate every band back to their "strong influence from the Velvet Underground," who was an ahead-of-its-time 60s rock band with elements of punk and new wave.

* Mention the quick rise and fall of the punk scene on the Bowery in New York, with a reference to how much you would have wanted to visit CBGB before it became so (sneer at this part) "mainstream."

* Sheepishly admit that you're "into the post-punk 70s bands like Talking Heads and Elvis Costello," even though "the Clash kind of ruined all that when they tried to be so commercial."

* Mention how "ironic" it is that in the late 80s, the predecessor to alternative music was called "college music," since now the alternative music scene is "obviously bigger in high school."

* Reference Nirvana's *Nevermind* as the album that took alternative music to the mainstream, leaving the bands alternative to those with huge airplay to be named "indie rock."

PLAYING HOLDEN CAULFIELD: PRETEND TO BE A LITERARY SNOB

* Express your anger at everyone who professes themselves a fan of *The Catcher in the Rye* but hasn't read anything else by Salinger. Finish with, "In my opinion, 'Franny and Zooey' is by far his best, but I would be open if you argued for 'Seymour: An Introduction.'"

* Mention your love for "George Orwell's nonfiction, where he really expresses his thoughts on the proletariat, even though so many people go wild about his novels like *1984* and *Animal Farm*."

* Reference the month you spent last year reading "the entire works of Kurt Vonnegut."

* Refer to authors with middle names or initials
  by a moniker: H.S.T. for Hunter S. Thompson,
  or J.S.F. for Jonathan Safran Foer.
* Express your fascination with Jack Kerouac's
  determination to be part of a poor minority
  counterculture when he was a privileged Ivy
  Leaguer.
* Buy your prop, or the copy of a literary snob
  book you'll be toting around with you, at a
  used bookstore so it's appropriately battered
  and dog-eared.

CAN YOU BELIEVE SHE BESPOKE THAT OUT LOUD?

If your French isn't fluent or native, that doesn't
mean it's okay to say Lewis Voo-tun while talking
about a classic brown monogrammed handbag. When
shopping, discussing fashion, admiring a magazine, or
complimenting a fellow fashionista, always use correct
pronounciation:

* *Hermès:* Makers of the Birkin and Kelly bags.
  Pronounced like "air-mez."
* *Louis Vuitton:* Designer with the most widely
  knocked-off handbags. Pronounced like "Louie
  Voot-uhh."

* *Cartier:* Fabulously expensive jewelry. Pronounced like "Car-tee-ayy."
* *Salvatore Ferragamo:* Comfortable loafers and status handbags. Pronounced like "Sal-va-tour-ayy Fair-ah-gahm-oh."
* *Yves Saint Laurent:* Handbags, clothes, and even a makeup line. If you can't say "Eve's Saint Laur-ahnt," shorten it to "Y.S.L."
* *Versace:* Wildly printed clothing. Pronounced "Ver-satch-ee" ("satch" rhymes with "watch" not "catch").
* *Pucci:* Psychadelic printed clothing, hipper than Versace. Pronounced "Poochie," which rhymes with "Gucci."
* *Moschino:* Gorgeous clothing and accessories. Sounds like "Moss-keen-oh."
* *Manolo Blahnik:* Shoes that cost as much as a laptop, but are so fabulous that they're worth every Benjamin. Pronounced "Man-oh-low Blah-nick."
* *Dolce & Gabbana:* Wild clothing, and this one may sound simple, but it's "Dol-chay and Gab-ah-nuh."
* *Christian Louboutin:* Sky-high stilettos. Pronounced like "Chris-tee-anh Lou-buh-tahnn."

* *Bvlgari:* Fine jewelry. Pronounced "Buhl-gah-ree."
* *Bruno Magli:* Leather shoes. Pronounced "Molly," not "Mag-lee."

And now for the more-commonly-found-in-your-local-mall-but-still-essential brands:

* *Zara:* Pronounced "Zah-ruh," and by the way, it's cheaper in Europe.
* *BCBG:* Clothing store with great dresses. The initials stand for "Bon Chic Bon Genre," and are pronounced as the French pronounce the alphabet: "Bay-Say-Bay-Jhay."
* *bebe:* Another French fashion brand. Pronounced "Bay-bay."
* *Lacoste:* Feeling preppy? Pique polo shirts for $75 a pop, this retailer is pronounced "La-cost" and does not rhyme with "coast."

SLANGUAGE BARRIER

NorCal may be hella cool, but Boston is wicked awesome. You can order a pop or a soda, wear Chucks or Converse, carry a pocketbook or a handbag.

But sweetie, why limit yourself to regional slang when there is so much more out there? Having a big vocabulary is a sign of intelligence, and it makes you sound sophisticated and places you in a position of power if you use words that are not commonplace. Who knows, maybe the term will gather popularity and become the next big thing at your school!

Before we can turn you into a debonair darling, it's time to fix some old nasty habits:

* **Listen to yourself** the next time you're chatting on the phone with a girlfriend, and keep a tally on a notepad of how many times you use the word "like."

* **Try to purge yourself of repeating the same phrases** over and over again. They may sound cute the first couple of times, but you're liable to drive everyone else batshit crazy if you can't find a suitable synonym.

* **Cut the crap.** Seriously, clean up your act. Cursing a blue streak isn't classy, and guys actually find it a turn off. If you only curse when you're really angry, your words have more effect than if you throw them around every time you realize you're late for class.

* **Enunciate.** For real, there is no such word in the English language as "tuh." You aren't going tuh school. You're going *to school*. If your

words are crisper, they won't sound rushed. If you take the time to form your words, people will take the time to listen to them.

* **Get rid of offensive slang.** You never know whom you're going to offend by complaining that having to write a three-page essay is so "gay," or by joking with your friends in the locker room that they better stop staring at your boobs, those "lezzers." As we've already discussed, there's no point in offending people unless you're doing it intentionally, or you might get an unexpected result.

* **Know how to turn on and off the slang.** You can "ohmigod" and "such a scandal" your friends to death, but don't expect your parents to listen to you if you can't speak their version of English at the dinner table.

Schools, like foreign countries, have their own set of laws, leaders, and language rules. At my high school, underclassmen often worked on their anchors during tutorial, but only because of block. What? In plain English, ninth and tenth graders used the campus-wide study period to work on their humanities semester essays, and the reason they had the time was because we had three long classes each day, alternating every other day.

You've obviously incorporated phrases unique to your high school into your vocabulary, as well as inside jokes with your groups of friends, so why not throw in a few words from somewhere exotic to balance your local flavor?

FRENCH

* *Je ne sais pas* (juh nuh say paw): I don't know.
  Friend: Hey, what happened to the last pair of Hudson jeans on the half-off rack?
  You (jeans behind your back): *Je ne sais pas.* Let's go hit the dressing rooms.
* *Chouette* (shoe-ett): great, cool.
  My boyfriend is so *chouette*, he put a rose in my locker today for our anniversary.
* *Teuf* (tuh-f): a party.
  There's going to be a small *teuf* tonight on the beach, but keep it quiet so too many people don't show.
* *Emmerdant* (eh-merd-ahnt): annoying.
  All Sara's talked about for the past week has been her prom dress—it's so *emmerdant*.
* *Bloblos* (blow-blows): huge boobs.
  Imagine running the mile in P.E. with those *bloblos*!

BRITISH ENGLISH

* Snog: make out with.

  Friend: Did you snog him?

  You: Yeah, we snogged for almost ten minutes
  in his car before he dropped me off home.
* Slag: slut.

  I'm never wearing this top again! My boobs
  almost popped out last period when I raised
  my hand and I felt like such a slag.
* Shite: take off the E and figure it out.

  Her mom grounded her for that? That's shite.

GERMAN

* *Beschissen* (besh-ice-en): crappy quality.

  Ugh, lunch-line chicken nuggets are so *beschissen*.
* *Klo*: bathroom.

  Ohmigod, I had to use the *klo* so bad during
  history, I thought I'd die.
* *Entspann Dich* (ahn-sh-pawn-dek): relax, chill out.

  Okay, so you got a B. *Entspann dich.*
* *Schlampe* (shl-ahmp): a woman who looks like
  she just rolled out of bed . . . either her own or
  someone else's!

  Did you see (so and so)? She's wearing mismatched
  sweats and looks like such a *schlampe*.

ITALIAN

* *Contaballe* (con-tuh-ball-ay): liar.

  He said he was with his family, but I saw him at the mall last night with some brunette. What a *contaballe*!

* *Figata* (fee-got-ah): cool.

  You got tickets to the concert? That's so *figata*.

* *Favola* (fah-vol-ah): fairy tale.

  Our first date was like a *favola*.

SPANISH

* *Sola vaya*: glad that's over, or good riddance.

  My last math test this month—*sola vaya*!

* *Paliza* (pah-lisa): annoying.

  My substitute homeroom teacher thinks we're all second graders. She's so *paliza*!

* *Borde* (boor-day): having a bad attitude.

  Stop complaining so much or people will think you're *borde*.

* *La dolorosa* (lah-dollar-oh-sah): literally, "the painful one," but is used to refer jokingly to the bill in a restaurant.

  Girl 1 to Girl 2 on double date: Do you think the boys will pick up la *dolorosa*?

* *Guay* (guh-why): cool.

That movie was so *guay*, too bad we have to wait a year for the sequel.

ALL ABOUT MOI

One of my many affectations is that I curse in Korean. In the beginning, it catches people off guard, and they ask me to repeat what I've said, and then tell them what language I'm speaking. After a while, my friends laugh about it and they tell everyone, "Oh, that's just Robyn. She speaks Korean." And then of course I'm the center of attention. People are fascinated, and they can't help it: Instead of being just another blond California girl at an invite-only soiree, I'm the only white girl in the room who speaks "fluent" Korean. They want to know all about me so badly that they're literally begging me to talk about myself. And you know what? The whole thing makes me feel like a *chun-jae* (genius) every time. (Of course, I only speak maybe two hundred words of Korean that I picked up during a summer job a few years ago, but just like which parts of my body I've shaved during my morning shower, that's not really information I share.)

If you've always wanted to learn a foreign language, why not buy a book and teach yourself? For practice, try out the phrases you're learning on your friends. You'll have the double benefit of feeling less self-conscious about speaking a foreign language and creating a sensation within your clique.

THE NAME GAME

Need to find a creative way to insult your sworn enemy? If you want to keep it clean and make her reach for a Merriam-Webster in confusion, here are ten words that mean "slut" in PG, SAT-level vocabulary:

trollop
chippie
strumpet
floozy
harlot
tart
concubine
hussy
slattern
wench

Need an adjective to go with it? These words sure aren't complimentary:

callous

heinous

loathsome

repugnant

revolting

vile

nefarious

déclassé

vacuous

vapid

Imagine the look on a teacher's face if your enemy rats you out for calling her a "callous chippie" or "heinous hussy." The teacher will be trying not to laugh!

HALLWAY SMARTS

So many adults try to differentiate between "street smarts" and "actual smarts," but in high school, it's all about the difference between "hallway smarts" and "classroom smarts."

If you're hallway smart, you know how to:

* handle yourself in social situations.
* gracefully recover from a faux-pas.
* understand when it's worth it to win an argument or to lose one.
* determine when you should speak up or keep quiet.
* turn a bad situation to your advantage.

If you're classroom smart, you know how to:

* define and calculate asymptotes.
* conjugate Spanish verbs in the imperative tense.
* perform a close reading of a sonnet.
* elaborate on the factors that contributed to American involvement in World War II.
* distinguish between prophase and anaphase.

The trick to being a successful social climber is finding your ideal balance between classroom smarts and hallway smarts, to balance a healthy social calendar with a heavy load of homework, to have study buddies as well as CW marathon buddies. So show off your book smarts as well as your magazine smarts, and your name will be at the top of every guest list and honor roll.

Gift Bag #2:
Access to the Sisterhood of the Social
Climbers' library shelves

From Regency England to post-millennial Manhattan, social climbers are the heroines (and sometimes heroes!) of their own novels. Find out how they fared in these classic and current tales of social woe and status quo.

Vanity Fair, by William Makepeace Thackeray
Orphaned Rebecca Sharp is driven by her social ambition to deceive her way into money and favor in English society.

The It-Girl, created by Cecily Von Ziegesar
Middle-class Jenny Humphrey tries to reinvent herself into an It Girl at her new posh boarding school after leaving behind her life of unpopularity and surprising scandal at her equally prestigious Manhattan private school.

The Clique, by Lisi Harrison
Claire Lyons's family moves into popular girl Massie Block's guesthouse, and unfashionable Claire tries to

win her way into the coveted It Clique that Massie rules at their private day school in Westchester County.

The Great Gatsby, by F. Scott Fitzgerald

Poor Jason Gatz, after taking on the role of wealthy fun loving Jay Gatsby, tries to win the heart of beautiful Daisy, who wouldn't marry him before he made his fortune.

The Rise and Fall of a 10th-Grade Social Climber, by Lauren Mechling and Laura Moser

New student Mimi Schulman infiltrates the popular group in her Manhattan private school on a bet from an old friend and keeps a diary recording her progress toward becoming one of the It Girls.

Prep, by Curtis Sittenfeld

Midwestern scholarship student Lee Fiora tries to gain acceptance at her boarding school by observing her classmates a little too closely and pretending her roommate's appropriately posh items are her own.

Pride and Prejudice, by Jane Austen

Mrs. Bennett schemes to marry off her oldest daughters to the wealthy gentlemen who rent a nearby country manor, thereby ensuring her daughters a higher station in society than her own.

Be More Chill, by Ned Vizzini
Jeremy Heere, a high school dork, buys a tiny super-computer that sits in his brain and instructs him how to be cool and get girls.

Gossip Girl, by Cecily Von Ziegesar
On Manhattan's Upper East Side, these high school students don't need to social climb, they've already reached the top of their school's A-list.

Private, by Kate Brian
After winning a scholarship to the prestigious Easton Academy, Reed Brennan vows to do whatever it takes to break into the Billings inner circle: the most beautiful, popular—and conniving—girls on campus.

You could ask him
for coffee some night. It's
the nonrelationship drink
of choice. It's not
a date, it's a caffeinated
beverage. Okay, sure,
it's hot and bitter, like a
relationship that way. . . .

—Buffy the Vampire Slayer

CHAPTER

3

Boyfriends Forever?

How to cyber-stalk, sweet-talk, find, date, or fake
your perfect guy

Cyber-Stalking for Dummies

He's cute, he's sensitive, and he drives a MINI Cooper.
He'll leave notes in your locker that don't start with "Roses
are red . . ." He'll burn you CDs and text you good luck
messages before your weekly Latin vocabulary quizzes.
On your one-month anniversary, he'll have a dozen
sunflowers delivered to your first-period class with a
quirky card that reads, "These flowers may be seedy, but
I'm not. Happy anniversary to the girl who makes traffic
lights green with envy."

Except, oops, you guys haven't talked. You've just
gazed at him, dreaming up these romantic scenarios
where he doesn't try to get in your pants, and never has
bad breath, and plays great CDs instead of sports radio
in his car.

Time for some reconnaissance work, darling, to see if the cutie pie of your dreams is really worthy of your attentions.

Guys are just like library books: If you want to know what they're about, check them out. Before you go for it with any hottie, become a boy sleuth.

* **Find his profile** on MySpace and look at his interests to see if you have anything in common. Maybe you're a Red Sox fan and he's mad about the Yankees. You'll probably fight a lot. Or what if every one of his MySpace friends are girls wearing outfits so skimpy that they make thong underwear look conservative? Chances are your guy's a player, and we're not talking baseball. Look at the messages people left for him to see how his friends view this guy.

* **Get his screen name** and "AIM-stalk" him: Check his away messages to see where he is ("soccer practice, then Denny's with the guys" or "out with Sara, back lata, pimpz"). Maybe you'll discover that he has a girlfriend already . . . or a few. Or that he's the kind of guy who always puts up a movie quote for an away message that's from one of *your* favorite movies!

* **Bonus screen name scamu** Check to see if he's online before you call him for that big date, so you know he's home.
* **Google him.** He might have a blog, or a special talent you're not aware of (he went to performing arts camp last summer, for example, and won Most Likely to Be Famous in the camp awards ceremony).
* And there's always the good old-fashioned **asking people about him**, or getting to know him yourself.

If you like what you see, it's time to make him fall for you—hard.

Playing Hard to Get With

As a social climber, it's up to you to figure out how you want to tackle your love life. Are you just looking for a fun date to the dance, or for a long-term relationship? Do you want a summer fling to tell your girlfriends about, or a guy to make your enemy jealous after her monumental breakup?

Once you know what you're looking for, and who you're looking for, tackle your future relationship like a term paper.

First, you've done your research (cyber-stalking him and finding out all the details). Next, you've chosen your topic (let's say long-term relationship). Now it's time to write the introduction.

If you don't know each other (e.g., he's been in your math class for three weeks but you've never spoken), introduce yourself in a way he won't forget. Or, if he knows you already, reintroduce yourself.

Tip Jar

* **Start a conversation** with him based on his interests. Once you've got him chatting, pull back, leaving him eager for more. Tell him you need to meet up with some friends but if he finds out anything more about the movie sequel, to let you know. This way, he'll come looking for you next time.

* **Shed some layers.** It's as cheesy and original as freaking nachos, but it works. Sit down in the seat in front of him in a sweater, then take it off mid-period, revealing a shirt that shows your shoulders. Sweep your hair off the back of your neck and let him fantasize.

* **Tease him.** Hey, it worked for boys in grade school. Call him stud when you ask him what the homework was, superstar if he gives you some of his potato chips, and handsome when he gets his hair cut. If you joke with him, he'll feel comfortable around you and start to tease you back.
* **Snuggle.** Tell him that you're not flirting, you're just sleepy, and put your head on his shoulder. Of course, by mentioning the word "flirting," he'll think about you in that context.
* **Give him a compliment.** He'll be flattered that you noticed his neat handwriting or the way he always overpays when a group of you go out to a restaurant and split the bill. If you're sincere, he'll think you're sweet—i.e., he'll think about you.

What comes next? The first date. It can either suck, or go really well. It's up to you.

Dating, and I'm not even kidding, can in truth be *more* stressful than writing a final paper. You have to look perfect, say the right things, keep him interested enough to call you again, and know how far you'll go.

To take some of the stress away, it helps to plan a date outfit a few days in advance, so you're not running late because the only top that matches your calypso skirt is the one you wore—and stained—yesterday.

Sometimes a first date is a casual stroll through a trendy shopping area, or a trip to the beach. If you know you'll be walking, that means you need to wear comfortable shoes. Don't chance it in the latest killer Louboutin-like stilettos. Blisters make anyone act bitchy, and having to cut the date short because you can't walk anymore makes it look like you're making excuses to get away from him. Compensate for less fashionable shoes by baring a little more skin. Without heels, you can get away with showing more leg. And always make sure to wear a purse you don't have to hold. If you wind up getting an ice cream or he buys you a present, how will you hold hands if you're too busy with a clutch?

If you're at a loss for where to go, consider these options:

DATE	PROS	CONS	TIPS
See a movie in the theater	• Sharing popcorn, snuggling in the dark, and it's only going to cost $20.	• No conversation. Do you even look at each other? • What if he tries to put some skeevy moves on you?	• Pick a movie that he'll want to see too, and act enthusiastic. • Google the film to find out impressive facts.
Go to a school dance	• He has to wear a suit and bring you a corsage. • You have a nice dinner with your friends and their dates and you get to dance.	• He wears a dorky suit and forgets the corsage. • What if he has poor table manners or orders something gross? • He might be an awful dancer.	• Discuss coordinating his vest with your dress beforehand to make sure he doesn't show up in a cummerbund. • Be clear beforehand if you don't want to freak dance all night.
Dinner and a walk around an outdoor hangout	• Great opportunity for conversation! • You're enjoying each other's company.	• You have nothing to say. • He wants to play video games all night.	• If you're going to be near shops, resist the urge to try things on. • Don't make him wait.

DATE	PROS	CONS	TIPS
Go to a (kind of illicit) house party	• No parental supervision. • A plentiful supply of music, plastic cups, and mysteries behind unlocked upstairs doors.	• You become the object of gossip, scandal, or the target of a warring clique also in attendance. • He gets drunk and acts like a jerk. • You get drunk and embarrass yourself. • Your parents find out you went to an unsupervised house party and you get in major trouble.	• Have the number of a cab company in your handbag in case you need to make a solo getaway. • Set the alarm on your cell phone to go off a half hour before your curfew in case you lose track of time.

Unconventional Date Ideas

Don't know where to go on your illustrious date? Or have you successfully completed the first paragraph and are ready to move the relationship to the next point? Try these date ideas for a pick-me-up:

* See a stand-up comic or improv comedy show. They cost as much as a movie or dinner, and you'll both be laughing, which is always good. Just make sure the venue isn't for adults only.

* Watch a movie in the park on your laptop. Bring a blanket and snuggle under the stars, alone, in the middle of a field. Bring snacks.

* Check out the website of a local college for cool events. Maybe a famous speaker is giving a free lecture, or an a capella group is having a concert. Going to a college event is sophisticated and fun, but make sure you don't need a school ID to get in.
* Cook dinner together. Make something simple, like spaghetti and meatballs with salad. You'll spend time together in the kitchen, and then you can sit down to a romantic dinner for two—just don't forget to make dessert.
* Go "car shopping." You need a driver's license for this one. Take the newest sports cars out for a test drive and pretend Daddy is going to buy you a new car for your upcoming graduation. This way, you and the boy are coconspirators and you share an inside joke.
* Have a picnic in the park and bring cheesy board games. You can feed the ducks and kick his butt at Boggle, all for free.

A Comedy of Manners

Whether your boyfriend drives a beater or a Beemer, there's a chance he'll take you somewhere fancy. You might be a guest at his cousin's wedding, sampling fine cuisine for your three-month anniversary, eating dinner before a formal dance, or dining with his parents. In any of these situations, proper table etiquette is a must. After all, if you've ever seen *The Princess Diaries*, you know how embarrassing it can be to commit a culinary faux pas. You don't want to, for example, drink from your finger bowl in front of his grandma.

Tip Jar

* If you're faced with a confusing array of silverware, start at the outside and work your way in. The silverware sitting sideways above your plate is for dessert and coffee.

* Your water glass is on the right, and your bread plate is on the left.

* If you're at a loss for which utensil to use, watch what someone near you does and copy them. Unless, of course, they're doing something weird, like putting ketchup in their soup.

* When having dinner at your boyfriend's house, if his parents ask you to set the table, place the fork on the left of the plate, then the knife and spoon on the other side, with the spoon on the outside. The napkin goes under the knife and spoon.

* If you are at one of his relative's homes, it's always nice to offer to help clean up after a meal, and it wins you major points with the family.

To Pay or Not to Pay

We're not living in an age of chivalry, although sometimes it may seem like it. Guys still hold doors open for you and offer up their coats if you're cold, but when it comes time to ask for the check, you're right back in the twenty-first century. When do you let him cover the cost of the night out, and when do you step in? Read on to find out.

<u>HE PAYS</u>

* If he has suggested the place, such as a restaurant or specific movie (but you leave the tip or buy snacks).
* If it is a first date (but you still offer).
* If he has planned the date for a special occasion, such as your birthday, Valentine's Day, or your anniversary.
* If you're having dinner in a restaurant before a school dance (unless you've already agreed to go somewhere fancy and split it, or have an agreement that he pays for prom tickets and you pay for dinner).
* If he has a gift card (such as a Starbucks card).

WaitdIf he is saving for a car or isn't earning money from a part time job, keep this in mind and offer to pick up your end of the expense, even if he would normally pay in that situation.

YOU PAY

* If you have planned the date for a special occasion.
* If you suggest a specific place, such as a museum or a show.
* If you have a gift card (such as a book of movie tickets).
* If he has been extravagant recently and you feel like shouldering some of the cost.

YOU SPLIT THE COST ANYTIME
NOT MENTIONED ABOVE, SUCH AS:

* if it's a really expensive date, such as a theme park with an admissions charge.
* if you're buying concert tickets without a special occasion.
* if it's an inexpensive date, such as meeting at a smoothie place, where it doesn't matter who pays.
* if one of you has spent a lot of gas money driving someplace far away.

In the end, if you really want to pay, there's nothing wrong with offering. Just make sure the offer is sincere, because it's a turnoff if a girl offers to pay and didn't even bring her wallet. Remember that dating is expensive, and just as you and your boy will get to know each other, you'll both figure out your own method for when you (or he) will be picking up the check.

I Can't Hear You: This Relationship Is Breaking Up

Just like every essay, high school relationships have conclusions (unless you marry your high school sweetheart, but honey, have you read about the divorce rate?). Consider them inevitable, and handle them with grace. Do not:

* tell your friends that you're planning on breaking up with a guy. Never trust anyone with information like that.
* blog about your relationship troubles.
* break up with him in an e-mail or publicly— unless he has hurt you and you're trying to exact revenge, which is only acceptable in the most dire circumstances, so use your discretion.
* be a bitch. You don't need him getting back at you and telling the whole school that you're like an elevator on the top floor—ready to go down.

* give him his stuff back. That is so bad-movie-
esque. Keep it. Girl, you earned those CDs.

And you know what? Don't feel bad if he dumps you.
Everyone has, at some point, been dumped. Just look
how many celebrities are on their millionth marriages.
And maybe, I hate to say it, dating someone from your
school wasn't such a good idea after all.

The Rule of 21:
A Social Climber Never Reveals Her Age

Regina: Is he bothering you? Jason,
         why are you such a skeeze?
Jason: I'm just being friendly.
Gretchen:[whispers] You were
         supposed to call me last
         night!
Regina: Jason, you do not come to
         a party at my house with
         Gretchen and then scam on
         some poor, innocent girl right
         in front of us three days later.
         She's not interested. Do you
         want to have sex with him?

Cady:	No, thank you.
Regina:	Good. So it's settled. So you can go shave your back now. Bye, Jason.

—from **MEAN GIRLS**

You know all those crushworthy hotties in your math class who look like they fell off page 72 of the J.Crew catalog? Those tousle-haired preps with classic good looks, who French-kiss better in French cuffs, and sport summer-sailing-in-my-yacht tans? Those boys.

Yeah. They don't exist. At least, not in your high school. So if you're getting all worked up over someone else's too-fabulous-to-be-fifteen-years-old boyfriend, or you're crushin' on a guy who's never going to go for it, stop.

Do you really want to take on the drama of trying to break up a happy couple, or the hassle of making a guy notice how perfect you are?

High school couples change as fast as the merchandise at Forever 21. A publicly bad breakup can ruin your reputation, and trust me, the A-list is written in erasable pen. Just because your place in the social scene looks permanent doesn't mean it can't disappear like everything cute in your size on an 80-percent-off rack if you wind up getting dumped in homeroom.

The smart thing is to assume that most boys in your school are too immature to make good boyfriends—it's a truth universally acknowledged that girls mature faster, anyway.

Would you want to wear the same prom dress as someone else? So why would you try on the same boys who have been sized up and rejected by every girl in the entire school?

This is where Rule of 21 comes in. It applies to boys met outside the classroom setting: Boys met at parties, movies, bookstores, Starbucks, art museums and galleries (props if it's his exhibit). Be your own PR person and spin your image any way you'd like. If you look five feet eight in heels, you're not telling anyone you're that height. They're making assumptions based on your presentation. So be creative. Put on a mental pair of high heels and hope your alter ego can walk in stilettos! Need some more incentives first? I feel a top-ten list coming on. . . .

The Class Picture Is Not the Whole Picture

TOP TEN REASONS TO DATE BOYS WHO DON'T GO TO YOUR SCHOOL:

10. He'll never ditch you and sit with the guys

at lunch so he can discuss some stupid sports game.

9. Your friends never "forget" to tell you some majorly scandalous piece of news about him until *after* you've become a couple. ("Oh yeah, I thought you knew he was arrested last year. Whoops. My bad.")

8. His friends can't talk smack about you, because they don't know you.

7. He's a totally unknown factor. No one in school knows anything about him, so use this to your advantage. You can make him anyone you want him to be. Or make him up entirely.

6. Baggage-free boyfriend (no ex-girlfriends snarling at you in the halls).

5. If you guys fight, no one has to know—and there's no nasty gossip all over school that you're on the verge of a breakup.

4. You have an excuse to ditch Straphangers—

just tell them you already have plans with
your fabulous boyfriend!

3. Everyone loves a mystery. Having a boyfriend
   no one knows makes *you* more mysterious
   and desirable at your own school.
2. You can send yourself presents and pretend
   they're from him (now you have an excuse to
   buy those decadent Godiva chocolates).

And the number-one reason it's better to date
someone from a different school?

1. If you guys break up, you can pretend that *you*
   dumped *him*.

COLLEGIATE CUNNING

Of course, if you really want to social climb, there is
nothing that says mature, sophisticated, glamour girl
more than a college boyfriend. And nothing's more
fun than trying to convince a college boy that you're a
college girl, because when they think college girl, they
think college girlfriend. This is where the age thing
comes in.

Age? A woman never tells. Instead, ask him what

"year" he is first. Then, when he answers, tell him the name of your grade, because those are the same in college. Be careful, though. There are a lot of differences between high school and college, and if you're going to fake it, you're going to need to know how to speak like a college coed.

COLLEGE COED-ESE

* Teachers are called professors. If you start to say "teacher" by accident, say "T.A.", which is the nickname for a graduate student who steps in for a professor (a teaching assistant).
* The caf is called the dining hall, and there is no lunch line. Usually, you eat on a "meal plan" or with "meal points," and choose from a salad bar, sandwich station, sushi, hot meals, soups, and pizza.
* Everyone has a major, or a field of study they concentrate in, but before you choose one, you're "undeclared," because you haven't decided yet.
* Classes have long, complicated names. Nothing is called "history" or "science." Instead, you might have "American Postcolonial History" or "Physics for Poets."
* If you need an excuse for why you couldn't

make it to see him yesterday (e.g., your mom got suspicious; you were grounded), you can always say that you got stuck waiting to discuss a paper with your prof during his office hours and there were a million people waiting in front of you, or that you fell asleep reading a reserve book in the library.

* Take-home work that professors give you isn't called "homework." In math, you'd have a problem set, or in science you'd have labwork. For humanities classes, professors assign "reading," which isn't graded. If you're taking an Intro to Shakespeare course, your reading for the week could be *Romeo and Juliet* (e.g., your homework is to read the play and be ready to discuss it).

* If he asks, your professor is either "brilliant," "pompous," "affected," "out of it," "ridiculously tough," "a boring lecturer," or "too busy writing his book to bother grading our papers."

* If a prof can't make it to class, the section is either cancelled or taught by the T.A. There is never a "substitute."

* Commuters are students who don't live in a dorm. They commute to campus from home or from their own apartment.

* Most people have classes as late as possible, and have no classes on Friday, so you'll have to complain about getting stuck with a Friday lecture if a guy wants to go out with you on a Thursday night because he thinks it's the weekend.

If this sounds like too much work just to date a guy your mother is going to say is too old for you, anyway, there *is* another option. . . .

How to Fake a Boyfriend

You are just too fabulous for guys to deal with! You're super picky about what your wallet looks like, and that only sits at the gum-wrapper-covered bottom of your purse. There's no way you'll ever be satisfied with the choices of guys to date. You need someone custom made, the perfect, handcrafted couture version of Mr. Wonderful. No guy is good enough for you . . . except Jake Doyfriend.

JAKE DOYFRIEND (IT RHYMES WITH "FAKE BOYFRIEND")

Seriously. Consider it. What's more fun than inventing the perfect guy and making all the boys you meet soooo jealous? The more incredible you make him, the more incredible *you* seem, because you're the lucky girl who got him. All those male friends on your MySpace profile will be rushing in to comfort you when you "break up" with Jake, and they'll be happy to talk you up to their friends in order to cheer you up.

First, you have to meet Jake. Make up his online profile, or take one of those 100 Things About Me quizzes that's always on someone's blog and fill in the perfect answers that the perfect guy would give.

Is he a sweet, sensitive poet or a dangerous rock rebel? Either . . . or both! Just make sure that you don't make him too unbelievable, or people might be suspicious if they Google him and get zero results. ("I thought you said he was in that movie *Mean Girls*, but I went to IMDb and his name wasn't on the cast list.")

FIVE THINGS TO DO WITH JAKE

1. With your camera phone take a picture of a hot (but unknown) model in a back issue of a magazine that no one reads and tell everyone that it's him.

2. Program a sibling's cell phone into your phonebook as "Jake," send yourself romantic

and flirty text messages from that phone, and then show them around at school.

3. Buy a boy's sweatshirt at a thrift store, wear it, and pretend it belongs to Jake.

4. AOL Instant Message someone who's a huge gossip at your school, type something like, "You are so sweet. I'm blushing as pink as the gorgeous flowers you sent me," and then apologize that you accidentally typed a message into the wrong chat.

5. Run crying into the arms of the cutest guy you see about how you had an awful fight with Jakey Poo and now you're (sniff!) siiiiiingle.

Like a Virgin

It's true: Most guys will like a virgin, and dump a slut. If you're going to go out with a guy in high school, chances are the relationship won't last. Trying to stay together (not to mention fall in love) while surrounded by gossip and popularity and bitchy backstabbing exes is really tough. Most high school couples aren't together long enough to actually, um, *couple*. And you know the saying "only fools rush in"? Well, honey, change that to "sluts" and you'll get the idea.

The real deal with high school boys is this: They have no technique. When they kiss you, it's all about getting their tongue in your mouth and hoping they can paw your boobs without being offensive. They don't have much practice, and they're so excited to be with a girl that they're selfish. Older guys do unto others, but teen guys want it all for themselves.

I'm not trying to talk you out of it because it's wrong, or because you're too young. Really, *they're* too young to make it worth your while. And besides, scheduling a time and place to do it is more difficult than an AP exam. You have to make sure your parents aren't going to walk in, you need to be safe, and you're going to have to fill your friends in on the details while swearing them to secrecy and hoping that your guy isn't blabbing about his score all over campus.

I'm not saying that you should rush out and buy kneepads, but there are other things you can do rather than *it*. The guys won't be very good at these types of things either, and the nicknames are a lot worse, but hey, I'm not your mother and I'm not telling you that you absolutely have to be a prude.

Just make sure you don't get caught going down, because social climbing is all about going up.

The Head of the Class

> For a kiss to be really good, you want
> it to mean something. You want it to be
> with someone you can't get out of your
> head, so that when your lips finally
> touch you feel it everywhere. . . . You
> can't cheat your first kiss. Trust me,
> you don't want to. 'Cause when you
> find that right person for a first kiss,
> it's everything.   —GREY'S ANATOMY

Sometimes guys think they're getting it right, but really, it's all wrong. Well, sweetie, I hate to break it to you, but it's up to you to correct them. Think of it as a favor to their future girlfriends, an act of charity, and a mandatory extracurricular for high school couples.

WHAT HE'S DOING	THE PROBLEM	HOW TO FIX IT
French-kissing	• Letting his tongue sit there in your mouth like a wet blob.	• Swirl your tongue around his until he gets the idea.
French-kissing	• Smashing his tongue in and out of your mouth so fast that it's like an electric sewing machine.	• Close your mouth and whisper that he needs to slow down because he's so hot, it's driving you crazy (i.e., lie, but stroke his ego).
Groping	• Clawing at your boob; squeezing your boob like it's a zit.	• Tell him, "This feels amazing, but I like it better when . . ." (i.e., compliment him so he doesn't feel bad about getting it wrong)
Making out	• Trying to go too fast.	• Tell him, "I liked what we were doing before," which makes him go backward instead of speed up.
Hooking up	• He places your hand on his fly.	• Remove your hand, place it in his back pocket, and squeeze. Optional: Whisper, "cute butt." A compliment takes the disappointment away.

Wait-List-Only Boys

Some boys are like status bags: coveted objects of lust with a wait list as long as a pair of unshortened Rock & Republic jeans. Like status bags, they're easy to spot. Just look for these three traits:

* Status boys, like status handbags, are gorgeous on the inside as well as the outside. I mean, have you ever seen the inside of a Prada bag? It's practically embroidered silk. Translated into boy, what you're looking for is a guy who's not only hot but fun to be around and interesting to talk to. Sometimes hot boys carry no status because they're so miserable and cocky to be around that it makes you feel bad, and in turn, people enjoy your company less. Just like carrying a knockoff purse, a wannabe status boy can be spotted by his less than desirable interior.

* Status boys are admired for a reason. Louis Vuitton has his signature monogram. The Birkin bag costs as much as a car. Chanel purses are buttery soft. What's the selling point that's got all the girls gawking at his window display? Is he a scholar athlete, the singer in a hot local band, the star of the school play, or the younger brother of a Hollywood celeb? After all, his high status has to come from somewhere.

* Status boys know what they're worth, and they don't lose their value once they've been used. Did you know that you can resell your used Fendi bags on eBay for hundreds of dollars

once you get sick of them? Status boys are the same way. They've been though a lot of relationships, but instead of being a "player" or a "male slut," they've still got girls ready to go to auction to bid on their affection.

AUTHENTIC OR KNOCKOFF?
HOW TO TELL IF YOUR HOTTIE IS THE REAL DEAL

AUTHENTIC STATUS BOY	CHEAP KNOCKOFF GUY
• Once you become a couple, people are jealous because your own status has just gone up.	• Once you become a couple, nothing changes except you have less time to spend with your girlfriends, who aren't impressed by your wonderguy.
• His exes are more popular than you are.	
• His exes are still friends with him because he's too cool to stay away from.	• His exes are missing in action or imaginary.
	• Everyone he dated seems to have gone psycho or moved cross-country.
• He's often complimented on his reason-for-status, and he accepts the compliments humbly.	• He fishes for compliments or acts incredulous when he receives any.
• He's affectionate in public.	• He acts ashamed or is self-conscious of being judged.
• He's polite when he meets your family.	• He freaks out and makes a fool of himself when you introduce him to your parents.
• He's interested in what you have to say and remembers what you tell him.	• He barely seems to be listening and sometimes forgets details about you (he orders pepperoni pizza even though you're kosher).
• He surprises you with sweet presents on holidays and small gifts for no reason (even mixed CDs count!).	• He asks you to bake him cookies or burn him CDs and doesn't return the gesture; he forgets to give you a present on your birthday/Christmas/Valentine's Day.

A status boy may not be the captain of the football team or the guy who drives a new BMW, but he's a catch because he makes you feel good about yourself. A girl as fabulous as you should never have to settle for some arrogant jock who just wants someone to make out with after games, or some pretty boy who owns more hair care products than your stylist. The ideal status boy is cute and fun, intelligent and talented, sweet and romantic. And believe me, if he has these qualities, he's got to be up there at the top of the social scene. The real question is, how can you get around the wait list and snag him for your own?

Breaking Up Is Hard to Deal With

It's not even your relationship—it's your friend's—but now it's your problem because she's called you sobbing about the jerk who broke her heart. Guess what? You need to be there for her. Girls remember when someone gives them a shoulder to cry on or turns a cold shoulder, and then they do the same. It might not be your crisis, but if you're a callous beeyotch, your friend will be the same way when you're sobbing into your cell phone a month later. So first, be empathetic and helpful—let her know that you're there for her. Then use these "empa-thets" to help her grieve and get over him:

* I'm so sorry. What can I do to help?
* Relationships aren't supposed to be easy, sweetie.

People change. I mean, look how much you and I have changed since we first became friends. But we've changed while still remaining compatible, and maybe that wasn't the case with Evil Ex.

* A gradual end to a relationship is way better than a fast fight. This way you won't think it was just that one fight, that one problem night when things got out of hand.

* Breaking up isn't like pulling off a Band-Aid— something to get over with as fast as possible. I completely understand that you need to take some time crying and feeling sad before you get back out there.

* No matter what he said, it wasn't you. Nothing is ever 100 percent someone's fault, and if you feel guilty, you're letting him have exactly what he wants.

And, alternatively, things you should never say to console a grieving girlfriend:

* **I never said anything, but I knew he was wrong for you from the beginning.** If you say this, then she'll think you've been lying to her, or that you let her get hurt. Ouch!

* **He was probably cheating on you, anyway.** Excuse me, Judge, I'd like that stricken from the record as speculation.

* **Now I won.t have to listen to you talk about
your boyfriend constantly.** Some things should
never be said aloud, and this is one of them. After
all, every girl obsesses over her boyfriend, and it's her
friend's job to listen—that's just the nature of being
girlfriends.

Boyfriendly

There are more reasons than downloadable ring tones
why a guy might not be your Prince Charming. High
school is the era of the unrequited crush, where guys and
girls have different ideas of what they're looking for in a
significant other, and what they can reasonably expect to
get. Geeks crush on populars, freshmen crush on seniors,
best friends crush on each other but are too afraid to do
anything about it. . . .

It's easy to get distracted by romance and forget the
ultimate goal of social climbing—achieving happiness
with your social standing through hard work and self-
improvement. Every girl wants a fabulous boyfriend, and
it will happen when the time is right. Trying to force it is
like buying that size 6 skirt at the mall when you're really
an 8, and it won't zip all the way, but you're determined
to make it work. And yeah, it may work for a while, but it
may betray you, ripping embarrassingly (and publicly!) at
the seams, or it may break way before seeing its fair share

of parties. So continue on your climb to the top of the social food pyramid, and if some eye candy catches your attention, by all means, take a quick rest stop for a yummy snack, but then keep on climbing that mountain!

Gift Bag #3:
A contractual agreement to put friends first and boys second, courtesy of the legal board of the Association of High School Social Climbers

The Social Climber's Bylaws Governing the Actions of a Good Girlfriend

Sometimes having a boyfriend feels like the most important thing in the world. Just like a huge test you need to study for by the end of the week, a boyfriend can be all you think about. And that is where many a Social Climber has stumbled on her way to the top. She becomes so consumed by the thought of her relationship that she is no longer likeable. Her girlfriends roll their eyes as she blabs on and on about Mr. Perfect, she never goes out on the weekends, and has too much on her mind to be there for her friends.

As a preventative measure, we at Social Climbers

Central have created this set of laws governing the actions of a Social Climber in a relationship. Once you read them, we will consider that you have entered into a written contract agreeing to follow these laws upon penalty of social status.

LAW #1: FRIENDS FOREVER, BOYFRIEND FOR NOW

In college, are you going to keep in touch with all of your ex-boyfriends from high school, or all of your best girlfriends? So make sure you're not burning your receipts, making an impulsive and unreturnable mistake. That is, don't ditch the girls just because a hot guy has fallen into your arms. Friends are there for you no matter what, and a girl with a great boyfriend and a posse of P.O.'ed former best friends isn't very popular. She's not very social. Ergo, she isn't a Social Climber. So keep your boyfriend close but your girlfriends closer.

LAW #2: DON'T PLAY BOTH ENDS AGAINST THE MIDDLE

If you complain to your boyfriend about your friends and then complain about your friends to your boyfriend, you're just asking for disaster.

LAW #3: LISTEN TO WHAT YOUR BOYFRIEND SAYS, BUT ALSO LISTEN TO WHAT HE DOESN'T SAY

"L" comes before "S" in the alphabet, but also in relationships. Your guy shouldn't be talking about doing anything sexual before he says he loves you. So be cautious that you're not being used before you rush in.

LAW #4: TELL YOUR PARENTS YOU'RE DATING SOMEONE, AND SET UP A MEETING

Mom and Dad are far more likely to be understanding about extending your curfew or shelling out big bucks for a prom dress if they know and like your boyfriend. And if they don't like your boyfriend, maybe your should listen to their reasons. After all, who's to say that your parents' judgment is so different from your friends'? Your friends may not want to hurt your feelings, but your parents want to make sure you don't wind up getting hurt.

LAW #5: BOYFRIENDS AREN'T A COMMODITY—NO TRADING!

Say you're dating a sweetie from Mock Trial Team. Okay, he wears crewneck sweatshirts, but he's a great boyfriend. Suddenly your stock rises. You can almost taste the sweet air at the top of the social strata. A-list status is nearly yours. So you cheat with a cooler guy, or look for a better boyfriend while still involved with Mr. Mock Trial. That's mean and unacceptable. The key to social climbing is to be liked and appreciated, and there's nothing likeable or appreciated about acting as though you're better than someone who cares about you.

Fashion fades,

style is eternal.

—Yves Saint Laurent

CHAPTER **4**

Fashion-Forward Thinking

How to be a fashionista on a budget

Pop Couture

Fashion-forward thinkers are never timid in their choice of ensemble, are gracious at accepting compliments and, like local weathergirls, can actually predict trends and dress accordingly.

But being a fashionista doesn't mean that you need to spend $500 on an outfit, or that you should run out and fake-tan until it looks like you're coated in Cheetos dust. Fashion is a personal choice, and what looks good on the most popular girl in school may look tacky (and imitative) on you.

Fashion-forward thinkers change styles like they change iPod playlists: skinny jeans and a chunky knit sweater one day, tailored black trousers and a vintage Victorian blouse the next. They mix Juicy with Salvation

Army, Old Navy with Stella McCartney, and own two dozen pairs of jeans, each tailored to correspond with the heights of their favorite heels.

Often, the media paints girls who love to shop as shallow and brainless, but if that's so, then why can I walk around Columbia University's campus wanting to ask nearly every girl I see where she bought her fabulous ensemble?

The only shallow and brainless girls are the ones who follow the trends like origami instructions, trying to mimic everything exactly. Without taking fashion risks, how can you show the world who you are?

Individuality in fashion is key. You may shop at Abercrombie & Fitch just like everyone else, but if you put things together in a new way, you're unique. You should aspire to be fashionable on your own terms, not merely "trendy."

The best part about being a fashionista is that you get to be an artist, and the canvas is fresh every day. Dress yourself up like a pirate in cropped pants and a billowy striped top, become a damsel in distress with a long, flowy skirt and wavy hair, or show everyone you're the boss in a fitted blazer and wicked stiletto boots.

Remember playing dress-up as a little girl? Fashion *is* playing dress up, except you get to wear the clothes out of the house—and they actually fit. So sit back, smooth the wrinkles out of your Diane von Furstenberg jersey wrap dress, kick up those vintage thrift store slingbacks, or just make yourself comfy in your favorite pajama bottoms, and consider me your personal shopper. From sample sales to thrifting to consignment boutiques, get ready to learn all of my fashion and shopping tips and secret bargain hotspots.

Shopping Remorseful, Shopping Resourceful

We've all done it. Gone into that 70-pecent-off sale at Urban Outfitters or that Nordstrom half-yearly sale and walked out with something we shouldn't have bought. Whether the purchase in question

* is a waste of money,
* fits great but looks ugly, or
* fits ugly but looks great,

there are ways to remedy this situation to make sure that your next shopping trip is well spent.

Tip Jar

1. Wear light-colored underwear. How will you ever be able to tell what that white lace dress looks like if all you can stare at are your black cotton briefs shining through?

2. Bring a strapless bra. Your boobs are a different shape and place depending on the bra, so trying on a tube top and tucking in your straps won't give you an idea of how it will really fit. You need to try the top on with a bra you'd pair it with in order to make sure you're not exposing a bra clasp in the back or buying something that flattens your boobs into trashcan lids.

3. Wear heels. You don't need to go all out with Sigerson Morrison four-inch stilettos just for a trip to the mall, but heels give your butt a lift, distributing your weight over a greater area, which makes your legs look longer and makes you look thinner. Everything looks better with heels. When shopping, wear a comfortable pair with a low or medium heel so you can see how skirts and dresses will really drape.

4. Wear something simple to get in and out of. You don't want to spend five minutes in the dressing room trying to unlace your corset top. Grab a tank top and a jacket, and comfortable bottoms (not sweatpants—please, that look is so trophy wife) and you'll be fine. At sample sales, there is often no dressing room, so you need to be able to try things on over your clothes, which is why a nice tank top and a denim mini is my preferred shopping outfit of choice.

5. If you're trying to predict the future, ditch it. If the skirt will look better once you lose five pounds, or the top is stretched tight across your chest (but if you wear a sports bra, it should fit), then sweetie, step away from the merchandise. Buy yourself something you can wear now, as you are, and you'll be much happier in the end because you'll actually wear it.

6. Don't be afraid to ask for a discount. If the most perfect tank top in the world is 60 percent off but one of the straps needs to be resewn on (and you're handy with a needle and thread), point this problem out at the

cashier and ask: "What is the best price you can give me?" You should receive an additional 10 percent off, making your purchase of a less than perfect item worth your time to fix it into something fab.

7. If it's the trendiest thing out there but the cut doesn't flatter you, put it back. When everyone was wearing those long babydoll tops and looking southern chic, I'd try them on and look knocked up. There was too much fabric for someone my size (barely five feet tall), but I didn't want to miss out on the trend. Eventually I found it, the babydoll top that flattered me. It had three extra inches of fitted fabric below the bust instead of just hanging limply, which meant that the overall cut was more fitted. Meanwhile, my Indian friends were complaining that they couldn't wear any of the embellished boho clothes because it made them look like they had just emigrated. Finally they started pairing rocker tees and Converse with the flowy skirts, and it looked great—edgy yet flirty. So shop around until you find a version of the trend that looks great on you.

8. Know the return policy. Some stores give you thirty days to make a return, while others only allow fourteen. You don't want to get stuck keeping your return because you missed the fourteen-day deadline.

9. Don't abuse chichi boutiques. It's fun to walk into Gucci and pretend you have all the money in the world, but if you mess up their dressing rooms and accidentally snag a silk top, not only will you not be welcome back, you might have to pay for what you wrecked. If you want to have a shopping fantasy day where you try on stuff you'd never pay for, do it in an upscale department store. You have a bigger selection, and you won't hog the store's only dressing room and leave the real customers waiting.

10. Don't feel that you have to buy something because your friend did. You're not keeping up. There isn't a contest to see who buys the most tops. If nothing fits, or you can't find the perfect pair of sneakers, don't worry. If you trusted your friend enough to go shopping together, then she won't judge you just because you put back

the Coach wristlet at the last minute. If you're shopping with an assertive It Girl and feel pressured, make sure you know the store's return policy, and make excuses when she asks you to go shopping with her again.

Retail Retaliation

> **Bianca:** There's a difference between like and love. Like, I love my Prada backpack, but I like my Skechers.
>
> **Chastity:** But I love my Skechers.
>
> **Bianca:** That's because you don't have a Prada backpack.
>
> —from 10 THINGS I HATE ABOUT YOU

I never shop retail. I used to, paying full price for a pair of Hudson jeans while dreaming of the legendary Free Prada Store, where Prada was so cheap that it was almost free. Then I discovered sample sales, resale stores, consignment shops, trading, thrifting, eBay, craigslist and yard sales, and I've never gone back.

EXCHANGE RATE

Imagine a store where 7 jeans, Gucci sunglasses, and Chanel bags are $50. I had only dreamed of a store like this too, before I accidentally wandered into one in L.A. Stores like Buffalo Exchange, Wasteland, and Crossroads operate on a "buy/sell/trade policy," which is why you can score that Chanel purse for $50 instead of the usual $1500.

Basically, customers bring in bags of clothes, shoes, and accessories they don't want anymore, and trained "buyers" go through the clothing and only pick out the best pieces. They give the seller 35 percent of what the item will be priced in cash, or 50 percent in store credit. But don't think that these clothes are all pulled out of someone's rejected clothing pile. A lot of designers, stylists, and people in the fashion industry unload great finds at these stores. The stock ranges from still-tagged current designer to worn-once-or-twice brand-name duds to gorgeous vintage finds.

I've bought brand-new C&C California tops for $12, vintage fitted blazers for $15, Lacoste polos for $15, Gucci stilettos for $40, and even cool jewelry for $5.

Buffalo Exchange has stores all over the country, not just in big cities, but if you don't live near one, they also have an eBay store! So start bidding on a $35 Marc Jacobs bag. What are you waiting for?

SAMPLE SALING THE SEVEN SEAS

L.A. may rock laid-back buy/sell/trade stores, but New York is all about exclusivity, and what is snobbier than exclusive designer sample sales? Some events are invitation only, where others are advertised in the Daily Candy e-newsletter, *New York* magazine's Sales and Bargains e-mail, or at topbutton.com. In a city where retail stores have a half-hour wait for a dressing room and sale racks never stock your size, the ladies in the know bypass Fifth Avenue completely and shop in warehouses and downtown lofts, paying cash and leaving with unmarked bags.

Sample sales are events where a certain designer unloads unsold merchandise from all the stores, samples and clothing worn by models, and even current season merchandise at a significant discount. Usually these items are priced at "wholesale," or one-third of the retail price, but occasionally can be found as low as 90 percent off.

WHAT YOU NEED TO KNOW ABOUT SAMPLE SALES

* There are either no dressing rooms or a communal dressing area behind a curtain. Plan accordingly.

* Absolutely no returns.
* Some sales only take cash, while others only take credit cards. Find out beforehand.
* If it's a shoe sale and they're only selling sample sizes, then you're out of luck unless you fit a size 6.
* It's best to look up the designer online before hitting the sale. That way, you know if the merchandise is current and if it's a good deal.
* Often, items are one of a kind, so take a girl-friend who isn't your size.
* Some sample sales restock merchandise daily, while others put everything out on the first day. Find out beforehand which is the case.
* Always sign the e-mail list at a sample sale so you learn about their next sale before it's advertised to the public.

Not all sample sales are in New York. Sales like Billion Dollar Babes or The Art of Shopping hit other major cities, so explore their websites, sign up for e-mails and, if all else fails, campaign for your next family trip to be New York City.

SAMPLE SALIVATING

I'll admit that I have a problem. When it comes to sample sales, I buy like I'm a Costco shopper . . . in bulk. First there was Calypso, this boho Hamptons retailer that sells $185 flip-flops and $200 cotton button-downs. I arrived at the sample sale an hour after it had started, and there was a line to get in. Once the elevator doors opened and I finally stepped into the warehouse, I had officially reached shopaholic's heaven. There must have been hundreds of cardboard boxes marked $5, $10, or $20. I took my time while other ladies grabbed embellished boho skirts from one another, swarming each new box as it was brought out. I snagged those expensive flip-flops for $5 (I bought three!), those button-down tops for $10 (I bought four!), a lavender silk skirt marked $200 retail for $20, silk camisoles and designer layering tops for $10 a pop (I bought four), a cashmere sweater for $10, and a metallic leather handbag for $30 (marked down from $300). Then I saw the wall of jeans. For fifty dollars a pair, I could have my pick of Hudson, 7, or Rock & Republics that still bore $175 price tags. The only problem? No try-ons. I already had a pair of Hudsons at home, so I knew my size. I examined the rise in the crotch and made sure the cut was flattering before taking two, one light wash and one dark. The line to pay was so long that it took an hour before I reached the register. I'd picked up more goodies along the way, and when the cashier told me it came to almost $400, I secretly freaked out but still handed her my plastic. When I got home, I took the items out of the bags and started tallying what they would have cost retail. The total was over $5,000 dollars. And when I finally got to try everything on at home, it all fit. When I wanted to go back again the next day, even though I didn't, I knew I needed help. But I didn't stop at Calypso. A few weeks later, Ralph Lauren had a shoe sale. I showed up late, and as I scanned the walls of $30-a-pair heels, I swore I wouldn't spend more than $150. Then I saw the boots. Buttery leather, knee high, heeled, laced, flat, and gorgeous. Every pair of shoes for sale was sample sized and I (don't hate me) just happened to have sample-sized feet. At $60 each, I decided I could have one pair of boots. Then some man in a business suit yelled out, "Ladies, the sale ends in an hour. All shoes are now $20, including boots, and all sneakers are two for $20." It was pandemonium. Everyone started grabbing, myself included. I snagged not one but five pairs of boots, four pairs of sneakers, two pairs of loafers, and three pairs of heels. I staggered up to the cash register with my loot and couldn't believe that I was only spending $240. When I got my shopping bags home, I called Mom, ecstatic about my purchases. "I bought fourteen pairs of shoes today!" I trilled. "Oh, honey," Mom said, "you didn't! Remember the Calypso Incident?" I cringed. "Yeah, but this was different." Actually, it wasn't. And in certain circles I'm still known as The Girl Who Bought 14 Pairs of Shoes in One Day. And they mean it as a compliment, a nod of the hat from one chronic shopaholic to another.

THRIFTEASE

I remember going thrifting with an alternative friend of mine before thrifting was hip. Back then, I could find three vintage blazers that fit me on one trip, three or four embellished leather belts, authentic 70s love beads, and Bakelite bangles. But now that the rest of the world has also discovered thrift stores, it's harder and harder to find good loot.

If you're going thrifting, keep an eye out for:
* Vintage vests
* Broken-in Levi's
* Heirloom jewelry
* Designer cast-offs
* Vintage belts

* Retro heels and ballet flats
* Fitted blazers
* Worn-in T-shirts
* Books (seriously!)

To find the best thrift stores in your area, look for the ones with the most frequent and largest donation centers. The more donations they get, the faster new merchandise is put on the racks, which means you won't be sifting through everyone else's rejects for the week. But be careful—when thrifting, make sure you don't buy something with stains or tears. Inspect all merchandise carefully.

CONSIGNMENTAL

I'm not a huge fan of consignment shops, where ladies determine the price for their unwanted clothing and get a percentage of the price once it sells. The prices are usually high, the saleswomen are snobby, and what do they have that you can't pick up on eBay, at a thrift store, sample sale or buy/sell/trade shop? However, what I love to buy at consignment shops are shoes. They're usually brand new or worn once, prompting their owner to get rid of them because they never found the right outfit to match or because there had to be more comfortable shoes to go with that right outfit. I once bought a pair of brand-new $400 Ferragamo riding boots for $60.

CONSIGNMENT CHECKLIST

* Make sure your item is a bargain—sometimes buying consignment isn't any better than waiting for the end-of-season sale.
* Make sure your item doesn't have any rips, stains, or tears—that could be the reason it got tossed.
* Make sure it's not dated. The store owner doesn't have to be choosy about what makes it onto her racks. And even though it's Prada and it's $30, that see-through raincoat is not still on the runways, sweetie.

Bonus: If you get friendly with the owner, she may save items for you or call you if she gets in anything from your favorite designer.

IT'S NOT PERSONAL, IT'S JUST SHOPPING

I kind of have a personal shopper, except not really. I blame it all on my ex-boyfriend's roommate, who showed me the Jimmy Choo sandals she'd just scored for $65.

"Where?" I practically drooled, and she gave me

the name of the shop that she'd wandered into. I didn't wander, I beelined.

It was a tiny box of a store in Little Italy, smaller than the bedroom in my New York apartment. There were no employees, just the owner, who stocked her racks with Showroom Seven finds and the discarded fashions of models, both print and runway. Unlike a consignment store, everything was handpicked. And there was always a sale going on.

The owner chatted with me as I picked my way through the maybe two hundred pieces she had in stock, all in small sizes. I walked away that day with a pair of Costume National boots for $40, and I couldn't wait to go back.

Over the years, I bought some of my favorite pieces from that store. I could never leave empty-handed. The owner knew me by name, and knew all about me. I knew when she was single, and how her dog was doing. She once set aside a pair of Alaia heels for me, and remembered everything I bought. My Burberry trench, current season, cost me $175 instead of $600. I bought a vintage custom-made black wool coat with silk buttons for $100.

Once, I made the mistake of telling the girls in my French class where I bought my "ohmigod, so fabulous" violet wool Dolce & Gabbana black-label skirt. On my next trip to the store, the owner told me how all of my "friends" had been by and almost cleaned her out. She said they hadn't been very nice to her, or wanted to chat.

I watched the ladies in my class primp with their new Kate Spade bags and cashmere sweaters, and in that moment, I swore never again to reveal the location of my most treasured shop, or send to my dear friend, my quasi-personal shopper, any customers who wouldn't respect the sacred bond of friendship between owner and fashionista in that tiny store. So sorry, girls, you may ask, but I'll never tell.

LOUIS FAUX-TON AND FAKE SPADE

There comes an important time in every girl's life where she has to make the big decision: whether to fake it or charge it. That is, whether to splurge on a designer handbag, or buy the cheaper knockoff version. I don't wear fake bags, but I don't mind girls who do.

FAKE AND BAKE

When I was a senior in high school, the big bag to have was Louis Vuitton.

One of my fashionista girlfriends bought three authentic Louies one weekend and became forever after known as the girl who had a Louis Vuitton for every day of the week (a slight exaggeration, darling, but surely it can be overlooked).

Everywhere I went, I saw signature monogram. I felt like the only girl in school who didn't have an LV bag. So I went to eLuxury.com and blew $450 on a Mini Looping-style Louis Vuitton.

When I carried the bag to school, the girls all exclaimed, "That's such a good fake! Where did you get it?" I asked them why they thought it was a fake, and every girl revealed that her bag was a knockoff—every girl except for my friend with the three authentic bags. I had assumed that since my friend carried real bags, so did everyone else. I was out $500 for a bag that my classmates assumed cost $50 in Chinatown.

Even crueler, when my dorm room was robbed during my freshman year of college, the thief, who took all of my handbags, left the Louis Vuitton behind. The handbag robber thought it was a fake too!

The moral of my little tale? If you're going to buy a trendy bag that's getting knocked off left and right, buy a fake. If you want to buy something classy, something that is stylish rather than the It bag of the moment, opt for the real deal.

HOW TO SPOT A FAKE

* You bought it in Chinatown, even though the seller assured you it was real.

* You bought it off a cart/the side of the street.

* It doesn't come with an authenticity card or serial number.

* The stitching is cheap and/or coming undone.

* The hardware isn't stamped with the brand.

* The inside of the bag is made from a cheap fabric.

* The zipper pulls don't bear the brand's signature.

If you really want to see how the fake bags measure up to the real ones, take a look at the authentic item in the store and write down a description in your notepad. Then take a look at that fake you're considering and see how it measures up.

	PROS	CONS
AUTHENTIC	• A status bag with all of the status. • Can be resold for a sizeable amount on eBay. • Won't fall apart.	• Costs hundreds of dollars. • You always feel like you have to be super careful with it. • Everyone might think it's fake anyway.
KNOCKOFF	• Looks like a thousand bucks but cost fifty. • You can afford one in every color.	• Falls apart easily. • Paranoia that everyone knows it's a fake. • No resale value.

FashionEASTa versus FashionWESTa

A blasé, black-clad Manhattanite sits sipping a mojito in the bar of some swanky hotel. She peers over the tops of her Chanel sunglasses across the room at a blond girl who has just walked in. The blonde is wearing distressed denim and flip-flops. Her top is floaty and soft, and she wears vintage jewelry and an oversize slouchy handbag. A California girl.

As L.A. is characterized by laid-back glamour, New York is the capital of sleek, sophisticated chic. Both looks are equally fab, but totally different. Are you a fashionEASTa or a fashionWESTa?

FASHIONEASTA	FASHIONWESTA
• Wears solid black during the day.	• Wears flip-flops anywhere, with anything.
• Navigates Park Avenue in heels, yes, even when going to the supermarket.	• Shops at flea markets and thrift stores for crazy vintage jewelry.
• Pops the collar of her polo shirt.	• Is never without her sunglasses.
• Wears red lipstick as a fashion statement.	• Carries an oversize hobo bag.
• Isn't afraid to rock a runway look that doesn't exactly translate to the real world.	• Is a blonde.
	• Hair is messy and beach-y.
• Carries a status bag.	• Considers jeans and heels "dressed up."
• Hails taxicabs with ease.	• Carries a status dog.
	• Knows how to parallel park on Melrose.

Shop Around the World

Whoever said money can't buy happiness simply didn't know where to go shopping.

—Bo Derek

A plain white shirt is fabulous if you casually mention that you bought it in France. Add "Parisian" in front of anything and it takes on a new level of chic. That boring no-brand denim jacket? It's your Parisian coat. Your three-year-old bikini? Your Parisian swimsuit, of course.

If you don't want to tell someone where you shop, or what brand you're wearing when they ask, shrug and proclaim, "I can't remember. Somewhere in L.A.?" Of course it helps if you actually do pick up some of these supposed cosmopolitan items on vacation. Check out these chic stops for the savvy vacationer:

NEW YORK
The skyscrapers stretch upward in sparkling glass and steel towers while the yellow taxicabs streak by

on the asphalt. From walk-up to co-op, townhouse to loft, Manhattanites are some of the best dressed in the world. Share their shopping paradise at these locations:

FIFTH AVENUE

Henri Bendel, a luxury department store, is just down the street from quaint Takashimaya, a Japanese luxury department store with unique triangular shopping bags. Walk downtown from there and you hit Zara, Mexx USA, H&M, and other European boutiques, including Louis Vuitton and Salvatore Ferragamo.

THE GARMENT DISTRICT

Sample salers' paradise, filled with wholesale-only purveyors of next season's look and warehouses with 90 percent off samples for shoppers in the know. An ongoing sample sale, Clothingline.com, stocks many great designers at a discount.

SOHO

Tiny boutiques and upscale flagship stores. SoHo stocks typical mall fare like Gap and J.Crew, but also dabbles in upscale shops like Kate Spade and Burberry. Side streets boast tiny boutiques with little known local designer labels at outrageous prices.

THIRD AVENUE
On the Upper East Side, Third Avenue in the 70s and 80s is a thrift storeper's paradise, with a half-dozen thrift stores all within ten blocks of one another. Uptown girls sometimes donate unworn designer duds, and if you can't find anything good, head over to MADISON AVENUE for consignment shopping.

L.A.
From Santa Monica Boulevard to Beverly Hills, this West Coast paradise is full of blond fashionistas, hot Hollywood celebs, and purse-size pooches.

MELROSE
Vintage and buy/sell/trade paradise, with upscale boutiques thrown in for good measure. Check out Fred Segal for the top looks of the season at top prices, and Fornarina for hot pumps and European sneakers with a built-in hidden heel.

VENICE BEACH

Small, beachy jewelry shops face the water, but if you want an outdoor mall, hit up the Third Street Promenade, with mid-range chain clothing stores (such as Banana Republic and Armani Exchange), accessories shops, carts, and a fun atmosphere.

RODEO DRIVE

The Fifth Avenue luxury brands in one convenient West Coast location. Completely unaffordable, but can you afford to miss being seen there?

CHICAGO

From the jazz clubs to the Cubs games, Chicago is as vibrant as the views from Lakeshore Drive, or the rides on Navy Pier. Let the Windy City's great shopping blow you away.

THE MAGNIFICENT MILE

This is the Chicagoland shopping hotspot, running along Michigan Avenue from the Chicago River to Oak Street. Amid the big-name retailers, boutiques, and specialty shops are department stores and two indoor shopping complexes: the Water Tower Place and 900 North Michigan Shops.

PAIVA

This store is located in the indoor mall Water Tower Place, and is an athletic fashion boutique, combining the best of active wear with brand names and current trends.

STATE STREET

Dotted with many historic buildings, State Street is home to major department stores such as Carson Pirie Scott & Co. as well as a number of younger and discount retailers.

HOUSTON

Breathtaking landscapes, a great music and theater scene, and year-round sunshine make Houston a hot-spot destination for everyone.

RICE VILLAGE

Near Rice University, this shopping district is home to the Village Arcade, with standard college-fare shops like Gap and Banana Republic, but also houses some unique boutiques that contribute to the Village's eclectic personality.

UPTOWN PARK
A European-style shopping village filled with boutiques and lavish gardens.

HARWIN DRIVE
This area is full of stores selling leather, clothing, jewelry, and perfume—all at great bargains. Pick up unique gifts for yourself or your friends.

BOSTON
From crew teams rowing down the Cambridge River to the sprawling New England college campuses, Boston's historic charm will make shopping feel like an educational experience.

NEWBURY STREET
Boston's main shopping street, Newbury Street, extends for eight blocks with its assortment of restaurants, many boutiques straight from Manhattan, and stores for just about everyone.

FANEUIL HALL MARKETPLACE
Home to more than one hundred shops and the Bull Market, a "fleet" of over forty pushcarts featuring unique wares from local artisans.

HARVARD SQUARE
Next to the famous campus, Harvard Square isn't a quad of academic buildings but rather an area of redbrick walkways that lead to hundreds of trendy shops, restaurants and bookstores, not to mention an array of street performers.

MIAMI
From South Beach to Biscayne Boulevard, Miami is a vacation hot spot but also a local shopping haven. Part resort, part college town, and part tropical paradise, the fashion here never fails.

BAL HARBOR
Upscale shopping worth a trip just to window-shop.

COCONUT GROVE
Beachy boutiques with the season's hottest clothing by top designers, local designers, and no names make up this district southwest of downtown Miami, in the areas known as the street of Mayfair and CocoWalk.

OPA-LOCKA HIALEAH FLEA MARKET
One of the largest flea markets in South Florida, with more than 1,200 retailers featured.

PARIS
From the scent of freshly baked baguettes to the Parisian woman sipping *chocolat chaud* in a sidewalk café, Paris is a breathtaking city. The sprawling architecture of the Louvre, the arching monolithic Tour Eiffel, and the lights of the Moulin Rouge all surround some of the best shopping in Europe.

LES MARCHÉ AUX PUCES DE SAINT-QUEN
It's the largest flea market in the city, so you're bound to find some chic vintage treasures to take home with you.

PRINTEMPS
The more affordable of the two big French department stores, you can find chic, lesser-known European-label fashion, as well as items by the store's own brand. Everything screams sophisticated Parisian chic.

RUE ALÉSIA
Outlet and discount women's fashion make this 14th arrondissement shopping area a little known haven of budget-friendly boutiques.

LONDON
Tan trench coats flap in the London Fog as the Tube rumbles through stations beneath the city. From the lush gardens of Hyde Park to the Gothic grandeur of the Houses of Parliament, Big Ben chimes the hour over the bustle of a city known for its fashion.

TOPSHOP
This teen clothing haven is the size of a department store, with sections for vintage, accessories, shoes, and denim. Get London's hottest trends at Urban Outfitters' prices.

OXFORD STREET
Great shopping with mid-range European designers and shops like Miss Selfridges, which has fabulous teen fashion and accessories at great prices, and Mango, a clothing chain with a designer look and affordable prices (think Zara).

PORTOBELLO ROAD

One of the most famous markets in the world, noted for its second-hand selection on Fridays and antiques on Saturdays. Check out the local galleries, arcades, cafés, and shops as well!

ROME

You may Rome around the world, but all roads lead to it. From the crumbling glory of the ancient Coliseum to the cool waters of the Trevi Fountain, this Italian city pulses with nightclubs and bright gelato shops, pasta and pizza and, best of all, a fabulous shopping district.

TRASTEVERE

A labyrinthine neighborhood of medieval shops with small, funky clothing boutiques and jewelry stores. Check out Fuori Orario, which has funky T-shirts, jeans, and reasonably priced leather jackets by smaller French and Italian brands.

VIA DEL CORSO

A mile-long main shopping avenue filled with clothing stores, shoes, leather goods, and housewares that run from antique to cutting edge.

If your world-traveler image is thanks in large part to the World Wide Web, make sure you're pronouncing the locations correctly. There's no harm in having a friendly chat about how the *moules frites* in Saint-Tropez are the best you've had, but you should be saying "mool freet in san trow-pay."

Fashion Forward, Fashion Backward

Plenty of girls parade around in Prada shoes and MAC lipgloss, but not all of them are social climbers. Some are just trendy, wanting to wear whatever's in style, waiting for magazines and other (more popular) girls to predict the trends. Some are It Girls who don't need to social climb because they've already reached the peak and have nowhere else to go but down (go on, give her a push and watch her tumble). But others are true Social Climbers, fashion-forward thinkers, and here's how you can spot them:

* She's a trendsetter, not just a trend follower. This girl may be wearing the same purse as everyone else, except hers isn't brand new, bought as soon as she was certain that she could jump on the trend bandwagon. She's been wearing it for a while, and maybe the strap is fraying a bit, or the leather is already pen-marked.

* She takes fashion risks un-self-consciously. Sure, wearing riding boots with shorts takes guts, but this girl makes it work. She knows she's pretty, so she doesn't need to show off a lot of skin or wear an outfit that will help her blend in with all the other girls. She wants to stand out, and she has the confidence to do so. Sure, her sunglasses are Chanel, but her earrings are vintage, and not everyone can get away with wearing a little girl's grosgrain ribbon bow in her ponytail, but she makes it look like it's next season's runway flair.

* She gives compliments that mean something. Have you ever received a hideous dress from your crazy Aunt Edna, tried it on only to find that it looked like a piece of sackcloth, and then rolled your eyes as Auntie gushed over how darling you looked? Yeah, not exactly a coveted compliment. But have you ever worn a pair of new I-splurged-but-these-were-so-worth-it shoes to school and had a girl who always looks gorgeous tell you that your shoes were fabulous? That's the kind of compliment that girls want to receive. If you can make someone's whole day just by telling her that her top is cute, then you, honey, are a style queen (and you've just made a new friend, you slick Social Climber).

Gift Bag #4:
An invitation to join the ranks of the
fashion-forward Social Climbers

The Social Climber's Vows of Individuality

Now that you know how to spot a fashion-forward Social Climber, it's time for you to take the vow to become one of us. So hold up high your triumphant tube of lip gloss, swear on your Manolos, and recite after me:

I am an individual. I wear what I like, and what I feel most comfortable wearing. I don't follow trends, I start them. I compliment other girls' style, rather than tear them down. Through fashion, I express myself, not just the latest issue of *Teen Vogue*. It doesn't matter if I'm wearing Prada or Payless, I'm still fabulous because I'm unique, just like a couture ball gown.

Let's break down these vows of individuality:

1. **I wear what I like, and what I feel most comfortable wearing.** True story: I've never

tried on a pair of thong underwear in my life. First of all, what's between my butt cheeks is my own business, not Victoria's Secret. When I pick out clothes, I make sure I won't have to wear a thong. Boycut, briefs, string bikini—anything but booty floss and I'm there. Sometimes, though, I break down and buy clothes and shoes that aren't comfortable. The Jimmy Choo pink pointy boots that made my toes go numb after ten minutes haven't been worn since. They're in my "To eBay" pile, along with the Miss Sixty jeans that really were too low for comfort. So, if you're tempted to wear something uncomfortable just because it's cute or it's what everyone else is wearing, ask yourself if this is something you're really going to get into, or if it'll wind up in the "Maybe Someone Else Wants This" pile.

2. **I don't follow trends, I start them.** Wear what you like, strut the sidewalks like they're your own personal runway, and sooner or later what you're wearing will make it onto the runway, as long as you're a fashion forward thinker.

3. I compliment other girls' style, rather than tear them down. Compliments, when genuine, are the best flattery a girl can get (or give). Girls love to be noticed, so notice them. Ask where the girl in your bio lab got her edgy new haircut, or tell your friend that her kitten heels are hot. Every time you feel like you want to trash someone for wearing tapered, sandblasted, high-waisted jeans, give someone else a compliment instead. If girls feel good about themselves, they'll like you as much as you like their cool bangle bracelets.

4. Through fashion, I express myself, not just the latest issue of *Teen Vogue*. Millions of girls read the same few fashion magazines each month, scanning the pages for trendy of-the-moment clothes to buy. Sometimes I read these magazines too, just to keep up, but I don't need to. All I need to do is go into some trendy shops like Forever 21 or Urban Outfitters and look on the racks (or at the girls who are shopping there) to see this month's hot items. But do I really want to look like everyone else? To buy what the fashion experts have decided to market to teen girls this season, after polling focus groups and consulting with their street teams? You can be your own street team and observe fashion in the real world to see where your style will go next. Getting suggestions from magazines is fine, but you should never feel as though you have to buy what's featured on their glossy pages if you don't like it or if it doesn't flatter you. After all, the leader of the group is never dressed the same as everyone else—everyone else tries to dress like her. *Teen Vogue* should be coming to *you* for their next issue's fashion focus.

5. **It doesn't matter if I'm wearing Prada or Payless, I'm still fabulous.** Really, fashion is all about attitude. If runway models just walked casually while chewing gum and digging in their purse for their cell phones, no one would care what they were wearing. It's because of their shoulders back, hips out, pouty attitude that their clothes look so good (and, frankly, runway fashion is like watching an art show, there's no way people would wear that stuff to the market to buy milk). So whether you've just thrown on a pair of jeans, flip-flops, and a tank

top to run out and buy Mom a birthday card,
or if your lip gloss matches your manicure and
your skirt cost more than your friend's Coach
bag on the way to a killer party, if you project
an air of confidence, people will believe it. If
the Olsen twins didn't own the fact that they
wore rags when they were college freshmen,
it wouldn't have been chic. By daring to
be different and by rocking granny clothes
like they were designer couture, Mary-Kate
and Ashley turned from cute straight-to-video
actresses into American fashion icons.

Well, maybe aspiring to be an American fashion
icon is a bit of a big dream right now, but who says you
can't be the style inspiration for your high school? All
it takes is a little bit of imagination, some great luck at
thrift stores and sample sales, killer bargains, the right
pair of shoes, and some attitude, and you won't just be a
fashion-forward thinker—you'll be a style maven!

[Home] is life's un-dress

rehearsal, its backroom,

its dressing room.

—Harriet Beecher Stowe

CHAPTER 5

Closeted Fashionista

How to tackle your drab bedroom
to make it fab

A Bedroom of One's Own

As a fashion-forward thinker, your bedroom should be just as fabulous as you are! Have friends over to hang out, offer to host study groups, get that hottie you've been crushing on alone behind closed (or locked!) doors. Your room should be an extension of yourself—sporty if you're an athlete; full of Broadway show posters if you're a drama queen. But first make sure your room is up to speed. After all, there's no reason for your realm of chic to be shoddy. *Quelle horreur* if it's filled with stuffed animals, childhood toys, or embarrassing photos of your awkward years! But make sure your bedroom expresses who you are. Don't paint yourself into a corner by going with a fashion theme if you've got to shove a half-dozen volleyball trophies onto the top shelf of your closet.

Treat your bedroom like it's your MySpace page and fill it with things you're into, a personal profile of who you are. This chapter is filled with ways to give your bedroom a makeover, from closet cleanup to maximizing your space if you share with a sibling. So read on to become your own interior designer.

Bin There, Stored That

Dress to impress is what I've heard, but I believe that you should dress to impress *yourself*. If you're impressed, you're confident, and other people will like and admire you. But first, the clothes. A bulging closet (or closets) is a must for any self-respecting Social Climber. How will you have an outfit for every situation if you only own one pair of decent jeans? I own seventy-five pairs of designer shoes, and I see nothing wrong with that. Organizing them, however, was a disaster. They lined the bottom of my closets, overflowed from their free-standing rack, stood at attention on my windowsill, and I still had pairs I couldn't figure out what to do with. Stashing my footwear showed me how to organize my closets. Here's what I learned:

* Off-season clothes go under the bed in storage bins. It's easier to pick out what to wear in

July if all of my tank tops aren't crowded by sweaters.

* Jeans are folded, with back pockets on top, so I can tell which pair it is without having to unfold. Jeans are too heavy and pull down the racks when hung up.
* I bought one of those hanging plastic tiered shelves from Target and folded a ton of tank tops and T-shirts out of the way.
* If you hang sweaters, they stretch into weird shapes and have little bumps on them from the ends of hangers, so fold them.
* I use a man's hanging tie-rack for my belts. It takes up no space, and I can find all of my belts easily.
* If you have a lot of scarves, screw a towel rack into the back of your closet door and hang the scarves over it.
* You can hang a half-dozen spaghetti-strap tops off the same hanger by looping the straps around the neck of the hanger.
* Reduce clutter by using colorful storage bins or containers. Did you know you can store shoes in stackable see-through plastic bins for easy access?

Decorous Behavior: DIY Diva

If your budget won't allow you to buy the entire contents of the Urban Outfitters housewares section, here are some do-it-yourself alternatives to splurging on your personal space. Bonus: Invite friends over and have a crafts night. You can have matching pillows or lamps in your bedrooms, plus you can split the cost of supplies!

<u>PILLOW TALK</u>

You'll need stuffing (for the pillows, not for Thanksgiving dinner, natch) and some oversized T-shirts. Check thrift stores for cool slogans or funny designs, or hit up Target in the men's section for cheap band shirts.

Cut two squares of fabric out of the T-shirts that are a little bit bigger than the size pillow you want. Now cut the perimeter into strips about one to two inches deep and one inch wide. With your two sides of the pillow together, take a strip from each side and knot it with its corresponding strip on the other side. Repeat until you only have three or four knots left to tie. Add stuffing, then finish tying knots. Trim knots to desired length. And there you go: a gorgeous, DIY throw pillow, no sewing required. You can add buttons, jewels, or silk flowers to make the design cooler, or you can make the knots with the fabrics inside out (remember to flip it right side out before you finish so you can stuff it!) to have a sort of keyhole look at the edges of your pillow instead of fringe.

LIGHT UP MY LIFE

Got a boring lamp that could use a makeover? Find a T-shirt that will slip over the lampshade and fit snugly. Cut the arms and neck off the shirt, creating a T-shirt tube top for your lamp. Now you can decorate if your shirt doesn't already have a design. Just be sure to slip the shirt off the lampshade first!

Tip: You can create a cool lamp by leaving a few inches of extra fabric hanging below the lampshade and cutting this fabric into strips. If you add beads from a craft store and then tie knots at the end of each strip to keep the beads on, you'll have an awesome beaded fringe lamp perfect for a hippie-, boho-, or gypsy-themed room.

WALLFLOWER

Instead of painting your walls solid hot pink, why not just paint the bottom three feet? You've still got a splash of color, but by leaving the rest of the walls white, your room looks larger.

STRIKE A POSE

Instead of a massive photo collage of you and your friends, why not pick a few of your favorites and have them blown up at a copy store into larger prints? Or, save the negatives (if you're not using a digi camera) and have them blown up to the size of a sheet of paper? Stack a few vertically on your wall and voil), a photo strip.

Theme Rooms

Are you known for being a star athlete, a diva, or a shopaholic? Have your bedroom match your personality and hobbies with some of these themes:

THE WORLD TRAVELER

If you've been to more continents than school dances, chances are your bedroom is filled with curios from all over the world. Show off your artifacts and photographs in style!

Check websites like overstock.com, target.com, and urbanoutfitters.com for foreign decor. Mix a vibrant Indian quilt with a Moroccan mirror and a Chinese lacquer side table! Turn your room into a Mediterranean bazaar with colorful fabrics, beaded pillows, and foreign statues. Pile bright pillows in a corner and hang up mosquito netting to create a Casbah hideaway where you can chill and do your work, or cuddle with a cutie.

Tip: If you don't have enough frames for your exotic photos, snag a long box (a tie box from Dad works) and fill it with sand or pebbles to anchor your pics in place.

THE DIVA

For the aspiring Hollywood starlet, turn your bedroom into a dressing room! If you can't fit a vanity, hang a mirror and vanity lights above your desk. Check party stores for decorations like plastic statuettes and cutouts of film reels.

Movie posters are available online, but the trick to making them stand out is framing them. Frames are available at most craft supply and framing stores. Or, if they're too expensive, check thrift stores.

Tip: Make a poster for the Movie of Your Life on your computer, get it blown up at a copy store, and frame it.

THE FASHIONISTA

Your closets are bursting with your impulse buys and amazing style! Your bedroom would look great with a fashion theme.

Buy a standing coat rack and use it to hang handbags! Tack squares of cork or a corkboard to the wall and use pushpins to display your jewelry so you can find it easily. Showcase your sexiest pairs of stilettos on a shelf over your bed.

Street signs for Rodeo Drive or Fifth Avenue add flair to your walls, and if you really want to get crazy, look for a mannequin on eBay or at yard sales and drape it with fabric to look as though your room is backstage at a runway show.

Tip: Instead of tacking magazine ads to the wall, buy a standing room divider that displays photos. Slip the magazine ads inside and voil), a far more glamorous option.

THE ATHLETE

If you've got more jerseys in your closet than dresses, if you drink Gatorade rather than mocha lattes, then your bedroom would look amazing with a sports theme.

Frame some of your old jerseys and hang them on the walls! Buy a chalkboard at an office or classroom supply store and decorate it with fake plays or use the board to keep track of your favorite pro team's season.

Make sure not to overdo the sports theme by having *everything* sporty. Instead, pick a color scheme and go from there. Match the frames on your posters and jerseys to your bedspread, for example.

Tip: Buy a hat rack to hang your ball caps, helmets, and glove for easy access.

THE MUSICIAN

If "notes" are something you play on the guitar rather than stash in your best friend's locker, then why not turn your bedroom into a concert hall?

Instead of tacking up posters of your favorite bands, why not decorate your walls with record albums for a vintage rock feel? Or, take the covers out of your CD cases and tack them up in a checkerboard pattern. Set aside a corner of the room to make your own tunes and keep your instruments and music stand there.

Tip: Find a microphone and stand on eBay or at a yard sale and you can feel like a professional when you practice, or have a great prop for karaoke night with your friends!

THE ACADEMIC

If your trophies are for debate tournaments and mock trial competitions rather than soccer championships, your bedroom should reflect your quest for knowledge! Think collegiate, and decorate above your desk with pennants from your top-choice colleges. Invest in a leather chair for your desk so you're comfortable when studying, and keep a shelf of games to exercise your mind—chess, Taboo, Apples to Apples, Scrabble. Make sure your bedroom doesn't boast too much. Trophies are fine to keep on display, but do you really need to have those certificates of achievement tacked to the walls? Buy a scrapbook to keep all of your A papers, ribbons and awards.

Tip: Hang up a magnetic board and magnetic poetry to play with during a study break, or make your own with words printed on computer paper, some glue, and magnets from a craft store.

THE SIBLING SHARE

Sometimes it's hard to ignore the fact that you're not Mom and Dad's one and only—especially if you and little sis have to share a bedroom. Here are some tips to make your space your own, even if you don't have a room to yourself:

* Turn your bed into a lounge by placing it with the long side against the wall. Line pillows up against the wall, and during the day your bed is a cool couch where your friends can sit and hang out if you don't want them to invade your sib's personal space.

* Loft your bed to maximize square footage. Think of all the extra room you'll have. You

could create a lounge area underneath the loft with pillows and beaded wall hangings, or set up an L-shaped desk area fit for an executive with a rolling chair and file cabinet.

* It's always good to have a lockable space where you can keep things away from your sibling—a new handbag that she's itching to borrow, or an iPod you've already retrieved from her backpack twice this week.

* You can divide the room to give yourself more privacy by standing a wardrobe so its side, not its back, is against a wall. With the doors opening to face your bed, you can have a little enclave to get dressed in the morning without reason to blush.

* Keep a decent-size mirrored cosmetics case on your dresser so you can put on makeup in the morning if your sib is hogging the bathroom.

Feng Shui Your Space

Feng shui (pronounced "fung-shway") is a design philosophy where the proper alignment of objects in your room can create harmony and balance. To clear your room of negative energy, check:

* Your bedroom door to make sure that it can open a full ninety degrees. Obstructions in

the path of your bedroom door symbolize restricted opportunity in your daily life.

* Where your bed is placed. You should be able to see the door when you are lying in bed so you have a sense of security and power over your personal space.
* That, when in bed, your feet are not directly aligned with the door—this is the corpse position and is very bad luck.
* That you're not sleeping under an exposed beam, which will cause things to weigh down on you while you sleep.

Bedside Manners

Extensions of yourself are everywhere, from the photos on your school binder to the decorations in your locker, to the interior (and exterior) of your car to your bedroom. As you become better friends with your classmates, or move it to the next level with a boyfriend, chances are these people will get to glimpse the things and places you surround yourself with. So let them see what you want them to see. Tuck away those photographs of you and your sixth-grade buddies if that was the year your orthodontist prescribed headgear. And hide that "Camper of the Year" plaque from the summer your parents sent you to fat camp. You can bring those memories out to share after everyone gets to know you for who you are now. After all, everyone has skeletons in their walk-in closets, darling.

The trick to having people accept your lifestyle accessories (car, bedroom) is having pride in what you've got. Your classmates can become jealous if you seem to be the girl who has everything. Instead, become the girl who has things with personality. Your car doesn't have to be luxury, but it should be you. The same goes for where you live. Sure, there are perks to having a sprawling mansion with a gated drive, but your home will seem more homey and welcoming if it's a simple split-level ranch house, or an attached townhouse. Just so long as you're proud of where you come from, and you've done the best with your own space, your friends will like it. Why shouldn't they? If you like it—and you're such an excellent judge of things (after all, you did become friends with *them*)—then there must be merit in your social accessories. So whether you've got a 400-square-foot suite with a balcony overlooking the ocean or you share a teeny space with your ten-year-old sister, make your bedroom as fab as your MySpace page by making it all about you!

Gift Bag #5:
An opportunity to find out what the members of the Sisterhood of the Social Climbers worry about

Sometimes it's frustrating how parents just don't get something. They don't understand why you need unlimited text messaging, or that nothing's going to happen if you get in a car with your friend who just got her license last week. And when you can't talk to your parents, that's what friends are for. They get you because they're going through similar things themselves. You share your crushes, your anger, and your worries. Here are three things that many Social Climbers worry about.

1. **Even if I'm nice to people, they won't like me.** It's funny, so many people go around thinking, *what if they don't like me* that chances are, if you're introduced to someone new, you're both thinking the same thing. If you let them know right away that you like them, they'll be so relieved that they'll think you're fabulous—and you are. So mention how much you enjoy talking

to them, how excited you are to have met them, and your new friend will find herself returning the sentiment.

2. This girl might remember something embarrassing that happened to me years ago and it would be awkward to talk to her. How many times have you avoided someone because your mom was driving you home from ballet, saw a sign for a yard sale, and when she pulled up at the sale and tried to buy some board games, it was at the house of one of your classmates? Or, you were in a Brownie troop with this one girl and she saw you cry in second grade at your first ever sleepover? The truth is that this girl won't remember, and if she does, so what? You didn't do anything to her. Everyone's had something embarrassing happen to them at some point. So what if this girl was there for your moment of humiliation? If she remembers and makes a point of bringing it up rudely, she isn't a nice girl and wouldn't be a good friend. So take a chance.

3. **My friend is introducing me to a friend of hers, and we might not get along.** Your friends are people you trust and like, so chances are that their friends will be nice. If they aren't, it's because they feel threatened by you. If you meet a friend of a friend, start with basic questions until you find a common interest. They should be answering your questions, not listening to you tell them about yourself. People feel more comfortable when talking about themselves, so get her to let her guard down and feel at ease around you. Tell funny stories about your mutual friend (never say bad things about her behind her back—or to her face, even in teasing), and make sure you pay more attention to the new acquaintance rather than your friend, so the other girl doesn't feel like a third wheel.

Never be the first

to arrive at a party

or the last to go home,

and never, ever be both.

—David Brown

CHAPTER 6

Party Planners and Hidden Agendas

Party planning and gift giving for social sceneristas

Swag and Swagger

Crystal glasses swirl and clink with each toast, the gourmet food is arranged with so much consideration that it may as well be hanging in an art gallery, and the murmur and hum of the evening is filled with laughter, snatches of gossip, and games of do-you-know-so-and-so? The party is so glamorous that the guests are given thank-you bags worth more than their designer formal wear.

Blowout bashes used to be solely the domain of Hollywood A-listers and Manhattan society, but now it seems that every girl's sweet sixteen is worthy of its own reality show.

Throwing a good party doesn't have to come with a hefty price tag. A little bit of imagination, a lot of class, and a few tricks can turn your party into an event to be remembered.

Jimmy Choose

First you have to decide what kind of party you're throwing. There are five types.

#1: **THE TYPICAL**

Christmas lights are strung all over the place, plastic cups overflow from trash bags, and liquor magically appears along with the football team. The CD player is pumping while some girl cries in the bathroom, a catfight breaks out, and something that belongs to Mom either breaks or disappears completely.

PROS	CONS	TIPS
• Rite of passage (stereotypical high school event). • It will definitely be talked about.	• A setup bound to attract crashers and drama. • It might be talked about in a bad way. • Illegal substances.	• Check the label on your top before you wear it to the party and make sure it's machine washable. That way if someone spills a drink on you, it's not a big deal.

#2: THE SWEET

Guests receive thick invitations written in elegant calligraphy and show up in dresses and button-downs. There is a sit-down meal and parents who alternate between standing in the corner looking stressed out and making sure nothing illicit is going on in the bathroom. This party takes place in a rented space, like a Bat Mitzvah or super sweet sixteen.

PROS	CONS	TIPS
• It's classy and you can have fun planning it. • There's a set guest list, and you know your parents will be around, so you won't be blamed if something illicit goes down in a bathroom or something breaks.	• It's expensive and can be cheesy if your relatives overrun the place or your parents insist upon a stupid theme (like the circus, or scuba diving). • Since you'll have invitations, everyone will know in advance who's invited — and who isn't.	• If your parents try to embarrass you (by giving a dorky speech, or having a slide show of baby pictures, for example), just smile and be gracious about it. Everyone else there has been embarrassed by a family member before. Let your parents have their fun — after all, they *are* financing the party.

#3: THE GET-TOGETHER

It's informal, really—just a group of girls watching black-and-white movies, eating raspberry couscous and herb-encrusted chicken, lighting scented candles, and falling asleep to a season DVD of *America's Next Top Model*. This is the kind of sophisticated party that can happen weekly with the right group of friends, where everyone rolls their eyes at how "juvenile" their classmates are being by hitting that kegger.

PROS	CONS	TIPS
• It's tasteful and informal, yet feels totally grown up. • It's exclusive and great for bonding. • If your girls' night goes well, it could become a weekly tradition for your clique, and you would be credited with starting the tradition!	• Your friends might turn the night into a cheesy "slumber party" with give-a-friend-a-manicure as the highlight of the evening. • It keeps people out and the few who attend could be no fun.	• Make sure you have a fun event planned to take place with the girls in a few days that you can use as leverage. • If they dare you to do something that would get you in trouble with the fam, you can always claim that you don't want to get grounded and have to miss next Friday's plans to ___.

#4: THE COED

It's at your house, and parents are there, but they aren't, like, *hovering*. A big group of girls and guys eat finger foods and swim in the backyard pool, rocking out to someone's iPod speaker system. Everyone sits around and watches the sunset in their swimsuits, gossiping à la *Laguna Beach*.

PROS	CONS	TIPS
• It's a pretty loose party, so everyone can have a good time without feeling like now is cake time, now is dancing time, etc. • You can have a big group and still be exclusive without offending people. • It's cheap.	• With such an informal atmosphere, people could wind up ditching the party altogether to do their own thing, or they could stay far too late and have to be kicked out by your parents. • Some nasty fights and gossip can go down, so watch out!	• Check with your parents beforehand about how many people are allowed over and how late they can stay. • Also, if you're going to order pizzas, arrange with your parents beforehand to see if they'll be paying, or if you and your friends will have to cover it.

#5: THE IMPROMPTU

It just kind of happened—a bunch of your friends met up at the movies, then decided to hit your house afterward and just "hang." You aren't prepared, the place is a mess, and everyone is chilling in the living room—i.e., chatting for hours while taking silly digital camera pics to upload onto their MySpaces.

PROS	CONS	TIPS
• No hassle of planning, no need to budget. • Everyone who's there when the party starts is invited, so there's no excluding friends by accident.	• You don't get to plan what happens, so the party is totally unpredictable (you didn't talk with your parents about this beforehand, either, and they may not be thrilled). • Maybe your best friend couldn't come out that night, and when she finds out there was a party, she gets mad at you.	• If some of your friends aren't there when the party starts, send them a text message letting them know what's going on. That way they can still show up, and if you run out of any food or drinks, you might be able to convince them to pick something up on their drive over.

Feeling Bashful?

Just like reading the covers of tabloid magazines in the checkout aisle of a grocery store, we can't help but obsess over parties: What to wear, whom to invite, what to say to people you do invite once they show up, what will happen once the party starts, who will crash, how it will end. When planning your fête, keep these ideas in mind:

THEME GIRLS

Even if you're just having a bunch of friends over to lounge by your pool, your event should have a theme. Are you going for a tropical paradise with virgin daiquiris and sweet fresh fruit, or a summer bash with pizzas and candy? A theme can be as simple as what you're wearing or where you're going: A day at the beach means a portable boom box and Frisbee, a day at a theme park means cheesy digi cam shots and funnel cake.

Of course you can go all out and throw an über-theme party, but there needs to be an incentive to get people excited. Spread the word about fabulous prizes for a costume contest or a dance off. Need some themes? Try these:

80s LADIES

Pop *Footloose* in your DVD player, put on your best pair of leggings and brightest off-the-shoulder top, and sing and dance along to the film. Throw an 80s dance party and costume contest afterward.

SKULL AND BONES

Watch *Pirates of the Caribbean*, have everyone dress as pirates or marauders, and go on a flashlight-led scavenger hunt. Make sure to have elaborate clues for the hunt, and it's best if teams have access to cars. Just make sure no one's knocking on your neighbor's door asking to borrow a pinch of sea salt—yawn. And how very third grade. The racier and more scandalous the items on the list are, the better.

FOR RICHER OR POORER

Give each guest $1,000 of Monopoly money when they arrive. Their goal is to get people to give them money for doing dares. The person with the most money by the end of the night wins. Have everyone dress in their finery, and let the games begin. Psst! I bet your crush would kiss you if you offered him $200!

FOOD CRITICS

A lot of girls in your school may be on some ridiculous diet, or may be vegetarians or kosher, so be sure to have some food options that everyone can eat. A few cute ideas:

FISHBOWL

Get some fishbowls from a pet supply store and stock them with Pepperidge Farm Goldfish. Fill one or two with blue-food-coloring-tinted water and a handful of marbles for a fishy-ambiance. Bonus: bowls of Swedish Fish.

VASE OFF

Find plastic vases and vials at a party supply store and fill each one with a different color of Skittles or M&M's. Bonus: Display them in rainbow order.

STAMPEDE

Cut a design out of a piece of paper like a heart or a star and place this sheet over brownies. Sprinkle powdered sugar. You'll have yummy chocolate desserts with sugar stamps.

SAY CHEESE

Setting out a spread of cheeses and crackers (and no, we're not talking Kraft Singles and animal crackers) shows volumes of sophistication. It is très European chic to serve a "selection" of cheeses.

GLASSES, NOT FOUR-EYES

Plastic champagne glasses can make pudding look gourmet. You can even layer chocolate and vanilla for a black-and-white theme. Just make sure you have spoons long enough to reach the bottoms of the glasses.

SUPERSTAR BUCKS

Set up a coffee bar with whipped cream, cinnamon, and biscotti. Giving your guests a caffeine fix will pump up the party, and who knows: With a set of bongo drums and the right attitude, you might spark an impromptu beat-night poetry slam.

> HAVE YOU HEARD? Evite.com can e-mail your friends invites to your party, providing them with an RSVP message board where they can see who else is coming.

Check-It-Out List

* Make sure you have an outfit to wear far in

advance, and make sure it's comfortable. You don't want to be the only one not dancing because your hot stilettos hurt. Although, if Andy Sachs in *The Devil Wears Prada* could run through Manhattan in Jimmy Choos, you can certainly suck it up, sweetie. But it's better not to have to.

* Stock your bathroom. You don't want to run out of toilet paper during the party and have people coming up to you and complaining about it. If you're serving finger foods, make sure there's extra soap around too.

* Talk with your parents beforehand. Make sure you agree with them on how much they'll be around—if at all. You don't need to stress over Dad thinking he's invited to challenge all of your guy friends to dorky arm-wrestling matches just because you weren't clear with him that he needed to respect the privacy of your party.

* Check the technology beforehand. If you've rented a DVD, make sure it plays and doesn't have scratches. Check the speaker hook up on your iPod so you know how loud it will go and how good the sound quality is.

* What's the ratio? How's the guy-to-girl ratio? If the party has more guys, it'll be rowdier, but with more girls, it'll be cattier. Look at your guest list for an idea of what to expect. Ten guys will eat way more than ten girls, so order food accordingly.

Party Planning

When should you throw your fabulous party? Whenever, darling! If you were a character in a GossipGirl book, would you need an excuse to throw a party? Be the girl everyone looks to for a New Year's bash, throw the post-prom get-together no one will forget, host a swim party on the first day of summer, organize a Secret Santa exchange, or just invent your own reason to celebrate.

If you throw annual parties, they'll gather their own buzz and you'll be able to sense the anticipation as the chosen date draws nearer.

Fête à Fête

Are you going to a friend's birthday soirée? Even if it's the most juvenile, eye-rolling, Mom-made-me-go party, complete with carrot cake, party hats, and a door-to-door-themed scavenger hunt, you should still exude sophistication and glamour, honey. Glamour isn't just about the way you dress, it's about presentation. So make sure you show up smiling and bearing gifts, and no, I don't mean a $15 gift card to Sephora, the ultimate generic gift that shows how much time you didn't spend picking out the perfect present.

Gifted and Talented Edification

The more unique or unusual the gift is, the bigger deal you are for giving it. And *quelle horreur* if you wind up giving your friend the same present that her random next-door neighbor bought. It shows people that you value them if you've given them something cool. Here are some untraditional gift ideas that won't have you plunking down a lot of cash each time a friend of yours gets one year closer to being legal.

1. **The Bohemian Writer Present.** Writers go on book tours, where they sign copies of their books. These tours are announced in Barnes & Noble newsletters, signs in bookstore windows, online, and in newspapers. Find a cool author's signing and get your friend a personalized autographed copy of their latest book. Add a small gift card to Starbucks and a pair of sunglasses

(Nordstrom has excellent ones for $10 each in the teen department, and Forever 21 also has some cool, inexpensive pairs). Put it all together and wrap it in black—of course. Your friend can be the coolest girl in the coffee shop sipping a latte in shades and reading a signed book.

2. **The Relaxed Chick Gift.** Give your friend a relaxing spa day in a box. Depending on how much you want to spend, buy either designer (Bliss, Kiehl's, Fresh) or generic (drugstore, Bath & Body Works) bath products. Add a scented candle and a small box of Godiva chocolates. If you want, add a mixed CD of relaxing music. Your girlfriend can spend a Sunday night taking a luxurious candlelit bubble bath with decadent chocolates.

3. **The Internet Savvy Present.** Is your friend a blogger? Has she done anything with her blog design? Pay a professional website design company in advance to design her blog any way she'd like. This can be surprisingly inexpensive. I had my blog custom-designed for $10.

4. The Pampered Princess. Send your friend a gift during class to make her feel loved—and to show everyone what a great friend you are when her classmates ask, "Who's that from?" Talk to the proper people in your school's office and have them send an office aide to deliver your bud a bouquet of sunflowers, a birthday balloon, a box of candy, a teddy bear and card, or anything cute you can think of. Your friend will be thrilled! Bonus: Send her a smaller gift for each class of the day, along with a hint of what the next present will be!

5. The "Extravagant" Gift. One of my girlfriends gave everyone Furla bags last Christmas. She told me laughingly that she'd found them at a sample sale a couple months back and stocked up. At 90 percent off, she'd gotten a tremendous deal, but it looked like she was lavishing money on her friends. So hit sales and if you find great items, buy in bulk and have a bag in your closet full of presents waiting to be doled out. I've given friends sample sale items before, like $20 cashmere scarves (usually $100), or Kate Spade pencil cases ($15, but usually $40).

Before you give away these fabulous gifts, make sure they're wrapped well, have price tags taken off, and come with cards. I prefer buying chic stationery-type cards at Anthropologie or party stores and hand-writing a message on them. The cards are actually cheaper than Hallmark (usually 10 for $18, or $1.80 per card) and they look more thoughtful because you took the time to personalize and didn't just sign your name. Writing a heartfelt card shows your friend that you value her friendship. Just don't make it cheesy, because that's sucking up.

Business Carded

I had modeled for my friend's magazine and was on my way to the launch party. My outfit was fab, my eye liner smoky, and my heels didn't hurt. I was all set, except I had run out of business cards. Quickly, I pulled out an old birthday card, traced a friend's business card to get the right size, and cut out six different business cards from that one birthday card. I wrote my name at the top in script, and wrote my e-mail address and website at the bottom of each card. When I got to the party, the cards were a huge hit. The society photographer was so charmed when he found out the cards were homemade that he took one to show his friends and shadowed me with the camera all night, calling me beautiful. I decided to make the birthday card business card my signature. It's environmentally friendly (recycling old birthday cards), the perfect thickness for a business card, and always gets a compliment whenever I give one out.

How to do it:

1. Grab some old birthday or greeting cards you have lying around.

2. Take a business card and trace the size, making sure not to mark any part of the card with writing on it.

3. Cut.

4. Personalize with your info (name, number, MySpace).

5. Hand them out. So glam, having your own card!

Bookmark Couture

Do you have a ton of shopping bags sitting around? Put them to good use! Take designer print bags (such as Burberry) and trace a bookmark on the bag. Cut out, punch a hole toward the top, and tie a ribbon. Instant designer bookmarks to use in English class, mark your place in your science textbook, or take with you to the beach along with those summer books.

Bonus: If you're giving your friend a book, stick one of these homemade bookmarks inside as a surprise.

Lotions, Potions, and Candlelight

Unless your friend practices Wicca, she probably won't be happy if you give her lotions, potions, or candlelight. These three are the Forbidden Presents, gifts you don't want to give or receive. Let me explain:

LOTIONS

Lotions can sometimes smell like strawberry barf or cause girls to break out in allergic reactions (if you give your friend hives, she won't be your friend for long, sweetie). Just like bras and panties, skincare products should be something that every girl chooses for herself.

POTIONS

No one wants aromatherapy oils or mud masks. These can also cause allergic reactions. Also, those cheesy "love potions" are nothing more than tacky plastic bottles of sugar water. What does it say about you if you actually thought to buy someone that junk?

CANDLELIGHT

Candles are the worst gift ever (unless one is part of a spa gift, in which case it is acceptable). First of all, they're a waste of money. You can buy candles at any thrift store, yard sale, or 99 Cent Store for what a lump of wax is actually worth. Second, a lot of parents won't let their daughters light candles unsupervised. And third, candles are something a girl should buy in case her boyfriend comes over, not a present meant to be wrapped up and tied with a bow.

Party Animal

The word "party" can mean so many things, kind of like the word "college," which can be an Ivy League university, a community college, an all-girls' school—you get the idea. A party can be a casual get-together, a raging kegger, a girls' night out, a sweet sixteen, or a supervised swim party. As long as you're a polite guest or a great host, a thoughtful gift-giver and a gracious gift-receiver, your party will be one to remember.

Gift Bag #6:
A free rental from the DVD library
of the Social Climbers

Just as social climbers are on the scene from New York City to L.A., they're also on the screen. New York may be churning out books about social climbing, but Hollywood premieres aren't shy on the subject matter either. Here are ten films, both classic and current, where social climbing is the theme of the silver screen.

Breakfast at Tiffany's

Audrey Hepburn plays Holly Golightly, a small-town girl turned New York socialite and escort searching for a wealthy older husband. Then Holly meets her new neighbor Paul, an aspiring writer and kept man. The movie glitters with fabulous fashion and quirky party scenes.

Say Anything

High school senior Lloyd is smitten with beautiful and unattainable Diane, and surprises everyone when she returns his sentiment. But Diane's dad doesn't approve and wants to break up the relationship. A great eighties romantic comedy.

Mean Girls

When homeschooled Cady enrolls in public high school, she makes a deal with her newfound unpopular friends to infiltrate The Plastics, the cool clique, and report back to them. But Cady is quickly becoming a Plastic herself as she deals with their psychological warfare and ridiculous social rules.

Clueless

Popular high schooler Cher Horowitz decides to prove to her stepbrother that she isn't self-centered by giving the school's new girl a makeover. But Cher is shocked when made-over Tai is poised to surpass her own level of popularity. Set in 90s L.A., this is an entrée into the hilariously shallow lives of wealthy valley girls.

Legally Blonde

Sorority president and fashion major Elle Woods is shocked when her boyfriend dumps her because she isn't "serious" enough. Elle tries to win him back by enrolling in Harvard Law, where social climbing is a combination of argyle, the right law firm internship, and learning to believe in yourself.

She's All That

High school stud Zach bets his friend that he can turn any girl into the prom queen in eight weeks. But when Zach gives art geek Laney a makeover and a social life, he finds himself falling for her.

Romy and Michele's High School Reunion

When Romy and Michelle receive invitations to their ten-year high school reunion, they realize that they aren't impressive enough and quickly try to fix their lives. But when that fails, the girls show up at their reunion in homemade business suits and claim that they invented Post-it notes. However, high school nastiness isn't over yet, and crushes, grudges, and unrequited romance all resurface at the reunion.

The Devil Wears Prada

Andy is a serious journalist who has just landed a job as assistant to the editor-in-chief of a major fashion magazine. If she wants to get her foot in the door of a big newspaper, she must scale the world of fashion where one false step of her borrowed Manolo Blahniks can set off her devil of a boss. This is what happens when the queen bee isn't just evil—she also controls your paycheck, and your future.

Moulin Rouge!

Christian is a penniless writer whose play is being performed at the legendary Moulin Rouge. Satine, the star, loves Christian but must seduce the evil duke funding the play if she ever hopes to escape her job as a courtesan at the Moulin Rouge and have a chance at being a real actress.

My Fair Lady

Henry Higgins, a language professor, agrees to a wager that he can't take a street urchin and make her presentable in high society. But then Henry's social experiment works a little too well.

If you come to fame
not understanding
who you are, it will
define who you are.

—Oprah Winfrey

CHAPTER 7

See and Be the Scene

How to blog, act, sing, or dance your way to infamy

As Seen in Reality

In today's society, celebrity is attainable, and being famous is definitely an option for the most driven, aspiring It Girls. Fame comes in so many different flavors besides Hollywood celebrity: the star athlete, the rock legend, the reality-TV contestant, the bestselling author, the gossip columnist, the girl about town. The path to fame isn't straight ahead. It's a full-scale climb for the social mountaineer, a choose-your-own adventure mad dash toward infamy.

So, darling, what do you want to be known *for*? So many girls sit at home dreaming of being famous, but not a lot of them ever decide *why* they'll be famous.

High school, of course, is a test drive for real-world fame. It's a preseason sale where you can get what you want early. Now that we've spent a while gossiping about ways to reach the top of the high school A-list, it's time to think big picture. From making your MySpace page glam to how to act if you become a celeb, from avoiding scams in the entertainment industry to blogging your way to infamy, this chapter will tell you all you need to confidently strut your stuff down the runway of fame.

Kiss and Blog

In the past, it may have been improper for a lady to kiss and tell, but these days, it's scandalous (in a good way) to kiss and blog.

A weblog, or blog, is an online journal, a web page that displays the most recent information at the top. The blog is filled with "posts," or short, instantly published pieces on a variety of topics.

I started my blog, Queued Paper, when I was a sophomore in high school. At first, I wasn't conscious of my audience, writing whiny little rants that were mainly for my own benefit. After a while, I turned those rants into short essays of the stupid things that happened to me: about my failed audition for the school musical, about the cake baking, movie-watching adventures I had with my friends. Suddenly I had a much larger audience.

I refined those essay-like blog posts even more, spinning myself as a character: an intelligent, witty, California fashionista obsessed with getting into a Good College. I mixed photos of my shopping trips to Saks with worries about college and eye-rolling commentary on my fellow AP English students.

Once I sold my first novel, my life suddenly became more glamorous. I was living in New York, going to parties, and hanging out with literati. I blogged it all.

By my sophomore year of college, my blog was well-enough known that I was asked to speak on a panel about blogging at a conference that included Pulitzer Prize–winning authors and National Book Award Recipients.

I not only had the most popular blog on my college campus, but people recognized me on the subway or at parties from reading my blog.

"Sweetie," they'd tell me, sipping their apple martinis, "everyone reads your blog. It's huge."

I don't keep track of numbers. I'm afraid to. But I estimate that somewhere around 5,000 people a week check in at Queued Paper to see what's going on in my life. I've kept the same shtick. I'm still the quirky, fashion-obsessed girl I was years ago, except now a bit more refined, a hint more glamorous.

The truth is, these days, bloggers are famous. Even the GossipGirl books are named after the central character, GossipGirl, an anonymous society blogger at her elite Manhattan private school. Anonymous bloggers who have been "outed" have lost their jobs, or gotten six-figure advances for their tell-all memoirs. Some bloggers are famous for their honesty, or their sense of humor. But most of all, the point of blogging is that people listen to you. They read what you write and are interested in what you have to say. As a blogger, you are the It Girl, and everyone else is reduced to leaving lonely comments pending your approval.

A Mind-Bloggling History of Blogging

The first weblogs appeared on the scene in 1997 and 1998, and were hand-coded websites with dated entries that linked to other websites. These blogs belonged to web enthusiasts, computer programmers, web designers, and people who decided to spend their free time learning to code hypertext markup language (don't laugh, not everyone spends Sunday getting a French manicure and a latte).

In 1999, Pitas and Blogger launched sites with precoded platforms, making blogging accessible to

people who didn't know how to code Internet information. Anyone could blog.

Originally, blog entries focused on articles that they
linked to, providing a sarcastic and snappy commentary.
These blogs have since evolved into personal diaries and
journals, photo blogs, gossip blogs, anonymous blogs,
and even news blogs with readers in the tens of thousands per day, hosted by online blogging platforms such
as LiveJournal, TypePad, and Xanga.

Blingo

For the Internet-savvy Social Climber, here's a list of
terms to know and love when it comes to blogging.

* **Blogosphere:** The online blogging community.
* **Post:** A word, sentence, paragraph, or essay tradi-
  tionally containing links.
* **Tags:** The keywords the author of the blog uses to
  sort his or her posts.
* **Nanopublishing:** Instant publishing, a.k.a. blogging.
* **Podcasting:** Creating online audio content meant to
  be downloaded into a portable device such as an iPod.
* **Sidebar:** A box of information on the side of a blog
  that usually contains links or information about the
  blog's author.

* **Thread:** A string of related comments on the same blog post.
* **Flame:** An offensive or profane blog comment.
* **Flame war:** A thread of offensive blog comments, usually by multiple authors.
* **Lurk:** To read a blog regularly without commenting.
* **Audioblogging:** Posts containing soundfiles.
* **Friends-only:** A post that is visible only to a list of the blogger's "friends" once they have logged in to their own blog accounts.
* **Profile:** A short, online bio of the blogger, usually contained within a sidebar.
* **Userpic:** A small, uploaded photo usually appearing alongside the blog entry with a photo of the blogger or an image that relates to the blogger's interests.

A Blog Read Round the World

Okay, now that you know what a blog is, you're ready to create one. First you need to decide what kind of blog you want to have.

AN ANONYMOUS BLOG

Your blog may be famous, but you won't be. Not until you're discovered as the author and then offered a ton of money for your tell-all memoir, that is. If you want to create catty web content without taking the blame for it, this is the type of blog for you. Create a ridiculous personality, like East Side Shopaholic, and blog photos of your new designer clothes and photos of the "fashion don't" ensembles you see on the streets (with wickedly witty commentary, of course). If you're going to use this blog to social climb, you'll have to stage an elaborate discovery of your true identity once the site has a huge following, otherwise you're putting in a lot of work for everyone to aspire to be like the East Side Shopaholic, not *you*.

GOSSIP BLOGGING

If you read *Us Weekly* even though you already know everything in it, or if you just happen to overhear all the dirt at your high school, consider a gossip blog. Psst, we hear that a certain redheaded track star was re-enacting See Spot Run during study hall as she sprinted toward the bathroom with an ill-concealed tampon in her fist. Or, if you've got it bad for emo guitar players who drive vintage cars with fuzzy dice, rumor has it that this campus cutie still doesn't have a date to the dance—are you his Lady Luck?

Gossip blogging can get you noticed, but it can also earn you a cafeteria full of enemies. Never post nasty

gossip in your blog or you'll quickly lose your audience—
everyone will be afraid to visit the blog because they
might be your next target. This type of blog is best run
anonymously, or as a collective with a group of already
popular girls contributing who can share the blame along
with the envy of girls who weren't invited to join in. Be
careful if you choose to create a gossip blog, because you
don't want horrible rumors to be traced back to you.

DIARY BLOG

If you're going to go the LiveJournal route and blab about
your fabulous life, you better *have* a fabulous life or at least
spin it to appear like you do. Resist temptation to post a
cryptic one-line pity party after you've been dumped, or
to bitch about how you're in a fight with your best friend.
Instead, read personal essays by writers like David Sedaris
and Ned Vizzini to learn how to be funny and entertaining
when you write about yourself.

In a diary blog, you can't just report what happened
to you: I went to the mall with Sara today and we went
to Sephora and bought lip gloss and then the food court
for Chinese food and after that we hit Abercrombie and
nothing fit, so we went home. That's boring. You can read
that anywhere.

What you can't read anywhere is: When S.

insisted on going into Sephora today, I almost died. My brother's psycho ex-girlfriend works there, and technically their breakup was my fault. I casually mentioned the term "employee discount" one night, and she totally flipped.

That's interesting. It's not just a grocery list of what you did, it's a situation that your reader wants to know how you handled. If you turn yourself into a character in your blog and record your adventures as though each post is a separate episode, then everyone in your grade will be tuning in to your life on the web daily.

THE CULTURE BLOG

The culture blog is a magazine without advertisements. You link to interesting articles about celebs—with biting commentary of your own, of course—you forecast fashion, throw in upcoming events for the weekend, and even blog photos you take of cute couples at the Winter Formal. The culture blog takes time to produce, and mainstream blogs with similar content, like Gawker, have numerous staffers. Consider starting a culture blog as a collective. You're in charge, naturally, and you can pick contributors from each grade or from different cliques to help create content.

THE EVERYONE-ELSE'S-BLOG BLOG

Maybe you don't want to have your own blog, but you know three dozen of your classmates who feel otherwise. Why not syndicate their blogs as LiveJournal feeds, creating a "friends list" that displays the most recent entries from every student blog on your campus? Pass around the web address and you're golden, darling, because you're the go-to girl who made cybergossip and classmate blog stalking possible.

MYSPACE IS YOURSPACE

Besides blogging, there are other ways for high school drama to continue outside of the classroom, and other venues for you to pick up more Internet fans—mostly social networking sites like MySpace and Facebook.

I'm sure you're aware that these sites are networks of web profile pages where you can leave comments and messages, display your top friends, join discussion groups, post photos and songs, and meet guys who are only interested in you if you happen to be wearing revealing clothes in your profile photos.

Let's take MySpace as the example. It isn't exactly the cesspool of crazed teenage sluttitude that so many adults fear. A lot of famous writers, actors, and musicians have MySpaces, and you can friend them and send messages back and forth. But besides chatting with the rich and famous, Madame Social Climber, you can use this social network to your advantage and make your page as fabulous as possible, making yourself as fabulous as possible by extension.

MySpace Exploration: Do's and Don'ts

Don't: Display any content that could get you into trouble. A lot of adults (like your parents—i.e., the people who can ground you and take away your cell phone—and prospective employers) are onto the MySpace phenomenon. If you've applied for a summer job as a camp counselor, for example, odds are that you'll be Googled, if not by your employer, by your fellow counselors or your campers. Do you really want them to find a photo of you with smeared eye liner and bra straps showing, throwing back a shot of whiskey? Obviously not. My rule is that I think about every online decision as though I'm an A-list celebrity. Why would I make it easier for the paparazzi to get the dirt on me? I keep everything private so my fans don't know any better than to love me for all my fabulousness, blissfully unaware of my faults.

Do: Credit fake photographers on the bottom of your favorite pics. Let the world think that people are desperate to photograph you because you're one of the beautiful people.

Do: Keep everything classy. Having a MySpace with a repeating background of fuzzy kittens is not cute, it's a migraine waiting to happen.

Don't: Give away private information/gossip in comments or messages to your friends. Why put yourself at the mercy of your possibly-going-to-betray-you-during-a-fight friends?

Do: Send messages to all the cool celebrities on MySpace so they leave you comments on your MySpace.

Don't: Fill out your information in AIM-speak. Everything looks more professional if words have appropriate capital letters. do u get it??? Um, yeah.

Do: Make sure your MySpace name isn't something inappropriate like hawtsexykittenrawr1001 or xpotxisxhotx. Basically, keep the comments about your looks and your drug preferences to yourself.

Don't: Share your password with anyone. A friend who has your password has the capacity to ruin your life if you guys have a fight. Imagine a stolen MySpace identity and the damage it could cause to your reputation!

I HEART INTERNET

I love the Internet. It's not realistic to think that you can be discovered walking down the street just for being your fabulous self, but it happens every day online. Previously unknown blogs become cult hits, and random people become MySpace celebrities. Just be careful that the content you post on the web isn't going to cause problems if it's permanent—or discovered by Grandma—and you'll be fine. After all, darling, you may love the Internet, but can you trust it? Has it ever said "I love you" back?

LIGHTS, CAMERA, YOU!

Your legs are longer than the 7 a.m. line at Starbucks. Your smile is brighter than the valedictorian. You can cry on command, and not just because the 75 percent off Jimmy Choo shoes were all sold out in your size. If you sang on *American Idol*, Simon Cowell would get tears of happiness in his mean little eyes. If you signed your latest book in Barnes & Noble, people would sell autographed copies on eBay for ten times the cover price. You are a natural-born performer, a diva, a starlet, an actress, bestselling writer or a model. You just haven't been "discovered" yet.

The truth is, you're not going to be discovered, and sweetie, I don't mean that in a bitchy way. If you want to "get discovered," you better start by discovering yourself and then promoting the hell out of your newest client—you! There are stories about talent agents walking up to girls on the street and signing them, but those tales were created by the crafty girls who made it in the entertainment industry. They're decoy stories, and they keep the industry exclusive.

Haven't you ever watched a show on the Disney Channel (we all do it, just like leaving crumpled underpants on the floor before taking a shower, only we pretend we don't) and thought that you were a way better actress? Or seen a girl in a magazine and thought she wasn't that pretty? How about read a novel and wondered why that trash was even published? The answer is simple: Those people are privileged insiders, and you're stuck on the outside. But you don't have to be.

First, let's dispel some myths:

8 LIES, CHEATS, THEFTS, PROMISES, AND SCAMS TO AVOID

1. If you have to pay an agency/publisher/record company ANYTHING, they are scamming you! Even a "reading fee" or "consideration fee" of $50 is bad news. The real industry execs don't charge you—they take a percentage of what you make AFTER you get a gig, or they profit off selling your merchandise, such as CDs or books.

2. If someone comes up to you on the street and says they are an agent and you have what it takes to be "big," they are a total scammer. Like they don't get enough submissions from referrals and people within the industry who want to switch labels, houses, or representation?

3. If they want to photograph you in skimpy lingerie for a "test shoot," or charge thousands of dollars for headshots (which shouldn't cost that much even if famous celebutante photographer Patrick McMullan does yours

personally, in his studio, with a stylist and makeup artist to the stars), they're not legit.

4. If they've contacted you on MySpace or are running an ad on craigslist that says anything along the lines of "Want to be discovered?" or "Make $20,000 modeling for my website!" they're lying.

5. If they want you to take expensive classes with them for a lot of money before taking you on as a client, they just want your parents' money.

6. If they don't have a legitimate website and you can't Google them, even if they claim they are "just starting out," beware!

7. If someone will "give your demo to the biggest execs in the industry" for $500, don't trust them.

8. If you have to pay to post your headshots, résumé, demo, or query letter on a website that "people in the industry frequently visit

to discover new talent," these people have no idea what they're talking about.

IT'S NOT PERSONAL, THEY'RE JUST BUSY

People in the industry are busy! They are too occupied with their current list of talent to surf the web in their free time to discover the next big thing, or scan every girl in the crowd to see if her proportions are right to be the next Badgley Mischka model. They lunch with their clients, network with other bigwigs, attend conferences, launches, and premieres, and work with entertainment lawyers, publicists, and clueless interns and assistants. If they want to discover new talent who doesn't come "highly recommended" from a current client or personal friend, they will:

1. Hold an open-casting call.

2. Have "pitch sessions" at conferences that you have to pay to attend (you pay to see famous people speak on panels and give lectures), where you can meet with a literary agent or publisher for five minutes and tell them about yourself and what you've written.

3. Call a newspaper if you have been written up in it to obtain your contact information. (Reasons to be written up in a newspaper include: having your own column, winning a battle of the bands, an article on your high school's fashion show, play, or musical, a piece on your award-winning cheerleading squad or school choir.)

SNEAKY CHEATS AT DUCKING BEHIND THE VELVET ROPE OF THE ENTERTAINMENT INDUSTRY

* Date someone famous. Oh honey, we've all dreamt about it. And maybe Nick Lachey isn't a realistic option, but those Abercrombie models are kind of hot. There are some gorgeous, sensitive singers out there, and even some of the guys on MTV reality shows are looking kind of good. Heirs to huge fortunes are also famous if the money is big enough (but darling, that's gold digging, unless you two are the only fifteen-year-olds in your prep school who can quote long passages of your favorite book ever, *This Side of Paradise*, by F. Scott Fitzgerald, in which case it's fate).

* Sneak into events like Fashion Week and movie premieres and chat with people (not about how desperate you are to be famous) until they think you're charming and give you their business card. Ask your family members if they know anyone—you'd be surprised. Maybe your cousin's ex-boyfriend used to work at MTV.
* E-mail or MySpace-message someone you admire and see if you can strike up a friendship.
* Get a summer internship. If you've always wanted to write for a magazine, intern for *Seventeen* and volunteer to write an article if they're in a crunch.
* Be an extra. Check your local paper's classifieds or arts and entertainment sections for ads for jobs as a movie extra . . . which is essentially standing in the background for five seconds after standing around the set for two days, and you don't get paid, but if the director needs someone to say a line and they pick you, you get paid AND you get your SAG card.

A SAG card means that you've had a speaking role in a film, and that you are a member of the Screen Actors Guild. This means you get paid money if you're ever an extra, that you can audition for SAG-only roles, and that an agent is more likely to take you on.

To increase your notoriety, stand on the left in any photographs. That way, when the photo is printed, your name will come first, since names are always listed from left to right.

THE FAME GAME

You read in X magazine about *Veronica Mars* needing extras, and you were picked! You woke up at 5 a.m. on Saturday and Sunday, stood around the set bored out of your mind, and just when you thought you were going to go crazy unless you quit right that minute, the director asked if you could please say, "See you in class, Veronica." When the show airs, you have five seconds of airtime, AND a close-up on your gorgeous face. Welcome to the Screen Actors Guild! Of course everyone in school watched that episode, and the next day, even cool seniors you've never spoken to know your name. You go out after school with your friends (who, by the way, you have just surpassed in popularity—all hail the new CEO), and a girl at the mall recognizes you. "Omigod, weren't you on TV last night?" she squeals. Now that you're newly famous, here are some tricks to handle your sudden increase in notoriety.

OFF-SCREEN PERFORMANCE TIPS

1. Always be gracious, charming, and polite. There is nothing worse than a bitchy celebrity pulling a diva routine, and darling, you're not even that famous, so get over yourself.

2. Smile for the cameras, but let the paparazzi know when enough is enough.

3. Don't constantly talk about roles, parts, or jobs you've landed. Let people ask. If you volunteer the information, it sounds like bragging. If people ask you, you can sigh and pretend like it's top secret, and then talk about your fabulous self while they hang on to every word.

4. People will want favors, and it's your job to deny them. Don't give your friends a "leg up" in the industry. They may ask, but always respond, "It's so much more satisfying to make it on your own. And don't worry, with your talent, you'll be the next big thing any second." Because, seriously, do you want your friends to dethrone you? Use discretion, though, about helping out a select best friend, which could be a blast.

5. Invest in a pair of stunning oversize sunglasses for incognito trips to Sephora.

A Diamond Is Forever

I was in line at the campus bookstore trying to get my procrastinating hands on a textbook for class. It had been raining, and I was in my trench coat, sneakers and a pony-tail. A cute tousle-haired guy wearing a striped rugby shirt stood behind me, and we struck up a conversation. Before I knew it, we were exchanging phone numbers—despite my rainy-grunge look—and he really did call me.

We went to a dorm party together, a small "get-together," as he called it, but when we arrived, I could sense that something had gone terribly wrong.

First, the guests were draped over the furniture.

They didn't sit on chairs, they sprawled. Everyone was smoking cigarettes. And they all looked, oddly enough, like magazine ad people.

None of the guys wore Levi's and sweatshirts. Instead, their jeans were designer and their button-down shirts had collar stays or cufflinks. I didn't see a girl in flip-flops or a T-shirt. Instead, they all wore stilettos and cashmere.

"You have such great style," a girl drawled as we were introduced.

"Thank you," I said, tugging self-consciously on my 80 percent off black bouclé miniskirt.

Why hadn't she just said, "I like your top?" I wondered.

I settled in and listened to everyone talk about their internships at Gucci, their spring breaks in Milan, and the Foucault they'd read, just to be pretentious. Then a debate sprang up over who was smoking the rarest brand of imported cigarettes.

It didn't feel like a dorm party. Everything was just too weird. And then my date introduced me to his roommate, last name included. Everything clicked.

This was the corner of the world where people's last names were brand names, where liking someone's style was preferable to coveting a specific item of theirs, where European vacations were planned and executed at a moment's notice, and for reasons as small as a four-day weekend.

And later that night, as I took in the new couches and plasma-screen TV in my date's double dorm room, I wondered what the people I'd just met would do if they ever had to work a dorky summer job with a name tag—but then I remembered that they never had to do those things.

It's hard not to covet a select spot among the beautiful people. Their lives—the wild and exclusive parties, the sprawling country homes, the gorgeous couples—seem like hot TV dramas without the drama.

Dreaming of a personal shopper at Barneys instead of sale racks at T.J. Maxx, a personal trainer instead of a sketchy gym membership, a private jet instead of economy seating by the toilets, and a more glamorous life in general is nothing new.

But beware that you know when to stop. Don't let socialitis rule you. Your ambition to be a better person in a more touted social circle is admirable, so long as you know how to cage your inner desires.

There is a reason that social climbing has tradition-ally had a negative image. It's because some girls enjoy the power they achieve too much and don't know where to stop. They social climb for purely selfish reasons, or just to see if they can get away with it. They date men they don't care about just to see what presents they receive. They have disposable sidekicks instead of best buds. They attend parties and desperately attach themselves to the most "important" person in the room. So grab your Montblanc pen—or your mechanical pencil with a chewed-down eraser—and go through this Socialitis checklist. After all, darling, only you can self-administer the cure for the socialite flu—a healthy reality check!

YOU MIGHT HAVE SOCIALITIS IF . . .

* **you hang out with people you don't like simply so you can say that you hang out with them.** It's not worth it. You'll have a better time around people you care for and get along with—and everyone will be able to tell. People gravitate toward positivity, and if your smile is glowing and you're having the time of your life, they'll be drawn to you no matter whom you're hanging out with. There's no sense in making yourself miserable—and for what? Status? Please.

* **you date to win, rather than to enjoy.**
  Sure, there are guys out there who will take
  you to their parents' ski chalet in Vail, but
  if you don't like your bf, then maybe it's
  time to sacrifice the black diamond slope.
  You'll be happier with a guy you genuinely
  like instead of having to psych yourself up
  for each date just to accept a new necklace
  or expensive meal from Mr. Extravagant.
  Besides, there are plenty of wonderful,
  generous guys out there you could totally
  swoon over, but how will they find you if
  you're already in a relationship?

* **you do things you don't care about just to
  make connections.** So, ever heard of peer
  pressure? And no, I'm not talking about Just
  Say No. It's easy to be tempted to choose art
  as your elective even though you really want
  to do drama just because your crush—or the
  most popular girl in school—has signed up
  for art. Why make sacrifices for an unsure
  thing? Yeah, you might become best buds
  with Miss Popularity, or she could hate your
  guts or laugh at your pathetic art. Do what

you like, and hey, you'll have an easier time making friends with people who share your same interests.

Are you starting to see a pattern here? Social climbing for the wrong reasons can turn into the Socialite Flu, which, if untreated, can mature into full-blown Socialitis, a permanent condition. You contract either of these social diseases from compromising your-self in order to achieve a higher status. By ignoring your interests and emotions, you are no longer striving to be the best version of yourself but rather to have people see you as better than them. So be sure to keep yourself in check, and your rise won't precede your fall.

Q-and-A List
Quizzes to Fill Your Social Quota

WHAT DO YOUR COLOR PREFERENCES REVEAL ABOUT YOU?

Pretend you've just walked into your friend's fabulous sweet sixteen party and are standing in front of two tables of party favor gift bags. You can take one of each, except the gift bags are in an array of colors. So choose one from each table, and then head on in to socialize!

Table one: yellow, blue, red
Table two: green, purple, orange

Which two did you choose?

_____

Now open up the gift bags and find out what they reveal about you!

* **yellow-green:** Whenever your friends need someone to talk to, you're the one they seek out. You are naturally compassionate!
* **yellow-purple:** You're an adventurer, always excited to try new things and experience new places.
* **yellow-orange:** You love to face challenges head-on and solve them. You're an innovator!
* **Blue-green:** You're a motivator, always encouraging people to reach for their dreams.
* **Blue-purple:** You're usually the center of attention, and people are naturally drawn to you! You're a starlet in the making!
* **Blue-orange:** You're a split personality, sometimes logical and sometimes creative, sometimes full of reasoning and sometimes impulsive. You're the best of both worlds!
* **Red-green:** You're a naturally calm person, and you keep your cool when things start to go wrong. You're reassuring!
* **Red-purple:** You love to plan events and are a natural leader. You're a director!
* **Red-orange:** You are your own person, and you're not afraid to express yourself. You're an individual!

ARE YOU MEANT FOR THE SOCIAL SPOTLIGHT?

When all lights are on you, how do you act?

1. Do your friends often come to you with their problems?

   _____

2. If you see someone who is uncomfortable (maybe a new girl, or a girl whose recent ex-boyfriend is in her homeroom), would you try to help them relax?

   _____

3. Even if you absolutely hate someone's guts, can you still acknowledge a positive trait or talent of theirs?

   _____

4. Do you enjoy meeting new people and getting to know them?

   _____

5. Are you usually positive?

   _____

6. If someone tells you a story, do you ask them questions afterward rather than immediately following it up with a story of your own?

_____

7. If you're having a bad day, do you restrain yourself from taking it out on your friends?

_____

8. Have you ever stood up for someone who was being made fun of?

_____

Now tally up your yes answers.

6–8 Yes: **Basking in the spotlight**

You really know how to handle yourself in social situations! Keep it up and you can't help but to leave a trail of friends and admirers wherever your Prada pumps will carry you.

4–5 Yes: **Definite glow**

More often than not, you really know how to work a social situation and wind up enjoying yourself as well, but you need to work on letting your guard down a little: After all, everyone is a potential friend until proven otherwise!

0–3 Yes: **Dim bulb**

Don't be afraid of conversations. If you don't show everyone how awesome you are, and how awesome *you* think they are, how will they ever wind up becoming your friends?

PLAYING STRESS-UP

I've been accused of being the biggest stress case in Manhattan. Believe me, constant stress is not a good thing! So check your stresses and make sure you don't let your worries grow to the size of an Olsen's Balenciaga bag: too big to carry with you! In the past three months, have you:

1. Taken honors or AP classes? (If yes, add 10 points.)

   _____

2. Had a leadership role in a club or sport? (If yes, add 15 points.)

   _____

3. Broken up with a boyfriend of more than a month? (If yes, add 10 points.)

   _____

4. Broken up with a boyfriend of less than a month? (If yes, add 5 points.)

   _____

5. Had problems with grades or issues with a particular teacher? (If yes, add 15 points.)

   _____

6. Moved to a new school or new town? (If yes, add 25 points.)

_____

7. Been injured seriously (a broken bone, for example)? (If yes, add 25 points.)

_____

8. Had a close friend move away or switch schools? (If yes, add 20 points.)

_____

9. Changed your appearance significantly (gotten a big haircut or braces, for example)? (If yes, add 10 points.)

_____

10. Worked an after-school job (babysitting counts!)? (If yes, add 20 points.)

_____

Now add up your points. What's your stress factor?

75 or more points: Serious stress

Wow, you should try meditation in order to take the edge off! How in the world are you supposed to be charming and fabulous if you've got all of these problems? You definitely need to de-stress.

45–74 points: Semi stress

You have some crazy things going on, but they're manageable. Try to stay positive, and maybe splurge for a massage at the mall, and you'll be doing fab.

0–44 points: Small stress

Wow, you have it pretty good! Your life is pretty smooth, so make sure to be there for your friends who don't have it as easy as you.

ARE YOU TOO MATERIAL?

> We're living in a material world and I
> am a material girl.   —Madonna

Sure, Fendi is fab and Dior is divine, but do you take your retail therapy too seriously?

1. Your best friend wants to borrow your favorite cashmere sweater for a dinner date with a guy she really likes. Do you let her?

   _____

2. Your wallet is stolen. Is your first impulse to freak out about losing the contents rather than the physical wallet?

   _____

3. Your boyfriend buys you a handbag for Christmas that you think is kind of cute— except it's by Exhilaration, which means it's from Target. Do you wear it?

   _____

4. If you found a $100 bill on the floor, would you honestly donate part of the money to charity?

_____

5. Would you be friends with a girl who wore dorky clothes if she was really nice?

_____

6. Would you date a guy with zero fashion sense?

_____

7. Is it stupid to cut labels out of clothes that are by "embarrassing" designers so no one raids your closet and finds out you shop *there*?

_____

If you answered no to more than one of these questions, you might be a material girl. And sure, there's nothing wrong with appreciating the finer things in life, but sometimes you have to be willing to settle for less. After all, if everything is perfect, you'll have nothing to joke about. And imagine the funny stories you could tell about a scenario surrounding each of those seven questions!

HANDY LADY: ANALYZE YOUR HANDWRITING

Ever heard people say, "It's not what you say, it's how you say it"? Actually, darling, how you write it counts too. So those flirty notes you scribble back and forth with your crush in chem lab are actually saying a lot more than you'd ever imagined. Want to know what your handwriting says about you? Grab a pen and copy this down in script:

Come, darling, my chauffeur will drive us to Jimmy Choo.

Fabulous! First take a look at your "m" in "my." Does it have rounded or pointed humps? Rounded means that you analyze things and consider the facts before acting, which are good qualities. After all, you can't just jump right into high school and expect to be well liked. You have to understand the game to play it. Pointed humps mean that you are impulsive and quick to decide. You know what you want without deliberation. Split-second decisions are your forte.

Now take a look at your "t" in "to." Is it crossed high or low? High signifies confidence and ambition, the marks of a social climber—hey, even your crossed "t" is trying to climb higher. Low shows self-doubt and constant evaluation, which are good, humble qualities, but don't forget to give yourself credit when it's due, sweetie.

Next, examine your "y" in "Jimmy." Does it have a fat lower loop, little or no loop, or an upstroke on the right? A fat lower loop means you are trusting and take what people say at face value. Little or no loop means you find it difficult to trust people and have your guard up. An upstroke means you gather stress and tension, letting it build.

Check out how you wrote "Choo." Are the loops on your o's leaning to the right? To the left? Is there no loop at all? Or are they double looped? Leaning to the right signifies that you are trustworthy and great at keeping secrets—and keeping to yourself. Try to open up a bit more, but don't betray anyone by blabbing their deepest, darkest secrets! Leaning to the left means that you have a cheerful demeanor—you're good at faking happy, even when you aren't. But don't keep your emotions inside too long. Double looped means that you are careful of others' feelings, and will sometimes tell white lies to protect them. Sometimes this can backfire! No loop signifies your honesty. You give your opinion openly and truthfully, no matter whom it will hurt. Be careful your big mouth doesn't get you into trouble!

Now examine your handwriting in general. Does it slant to the right, center or left? To the right means that you feel everything deeply and are sometimes ruled by your emotions. It can also mean that you are impatient. To the center means that you're a very balanced person and have a positive attitude, and also can mean that you are an independent person. To the left means that although you care a lot about other people, you tend to hide your emotions.

Take a look at the letters themselves. If they're wide, you're an extroverted, or friendly person. If they're thin, you're more of an introvert, or a shy person.

What about your capital letters? If they're short, you're modest, but if they're tall, you have a lot of self-confidence.

What about the spaces between letters? These show how heavily you rely upon your intuition. If all of the letters in a word are connected, you are logical and systematic. If only some of the letters are connected, you're artistic and intuitive. If most of the letters are unconnected, you focus on yourself and often believe you are right.

Last, the spaces between words. Bigger spaces mean that you leave yourself time to ponder, while smaller spaces show that you are impulsive.

Try the handwriting test on your crush to find out more about him. Pass him a note or have him write down the names of some of his favorite bands and then analyze away to figure out things about his personality he'd never tell.

WHAT'S YOUR PROM DRESS STYLE?

You've got a date, a limo, and a group of friends to go with, and now it's time to pick out your prom dress. Is your style more retro funky, classic, or trendy?

1. **Your favorite pair of jeans is:**
    A. Designer, and so expensive that you had to save for them for three months.
    B. Ripped and doodled all over.
    C. Dark-rinse, boot-cut Gap. Even though you own more stylish pairs, they're the most comfortable.

2. **You need a new pair of reading glasses. Which do you choose?**
    A. Whatever Prada's latest style is. So chic!
    B. Cat-eye rhinestone glasses. So glam!
    C. Tortoiseshell oval-framed. So timeless!

3. **You're at a thrift store. What's the first item you look for?**
    A. Brand-name items from current seasons. Hey, you never know who just made a donation!
    B. Seventies dresses for a crazy night out,

oversize baubles, and T-shirts with weird sayings on them.

C. Anything vintage glam, like antique jewelry or ladylike handbags.

4. Pick some music to listen to:
   A. The top-forty hits
   B. Janis Joplin
   C. Edith Piaf

5. Where would you like to go on vacation?
   A. Los Angeles
   B. Amsterdam
   C. Paris

Mostly A's: Of-the-Moment Trendy

You're a girl who knows what's in style, and what brands you'll splurge on (or wish you could splurge on). Forever 21 can't keep up with your pronouncements of this season's trends. Your prom dress should be of-the-moment, something that reflects this month's cutting-edge fashion. Try BCBG or Nicole Miller.

Mostly B's: Retro Chica

You're in love with vintage because it's crazy and fun and chic all at the same time. Vintage stores stock what you're looking for, a relic from the past that you can pair with insane leopard pumps, red lipstick, and a cool clutch, or go with a retro look from Betsey Johnson.

Mostly C's: Classic Glamour

You're into fashion staples and classic pieces that never go out of style. Pearls, a chignon, and an elegant gown will turn you into a glamorous starlet straight out of a black-and-white film. Try Caché or Sue Wong for your red carpet-worthy frock.

CAN YOU READ BETWEEN THE LINES?

In the classroom, it seems like text messaging is going on in every hoodie pocket and beneath every desk. But sometimes it's easier just to pass an old-fashioned note. Watch out, though, because people rarely say (or in this case, write) what they mean. Can you read between the lines?

1. **Your friend writes: Have you been talking to Jessica about me?**

    Does she mean:

    A. Jessica told me you were saying mean things about me, and I believe her and am mad at you, but I want to see what you have to say.

    B. I'm not sure if you've been talking to Jessica about me. Have you?

    C. Jessica is so not my friend anymore. Let's ostracize her!

2. **Your boyfriend writes: Have you seen X movie?**

    Does he mean:

    A. I haven't seen X movie yet, and hopefully you haven't either, and want to see it, so maybe we can go together this weekend.

B. I saw this movie and want to chat about it with you.

C. I saw you at the movies with your ex-boyfriend when I was watching X movie last night!

3. Your friend writes: Do you like (name of friend)?

Does she mean:

A. I don't like (name of friend), can I bitch about her to you, or do you actually like her?

B. (Name of friend) is a lot nicer than you.

C. Do you like girls, because I caught you staring at (name of friend) while she was changing in P.E. and, just so you know, I'm here for you?

4. A guy you're crushing on writes: What's up with you and prom?

Does he mean:

A. Are you into prom, because if you are, I'm thinking of asking you, but if you're boycotting the dance or already have a date, I don't want to ask.

B. Do you think prom is stupid, because based on what I know about you, you might?

C. I bet you're a horrible dancer and no one will ask you out and you will live alone with five cats whose names rhyme.

The answer in all of these cases is A. People may rarely write what they mean, but based on what you know about them or what they know about you, you should be able to guess. If you think someone has found out something horrible you did, and they're hinting about it, chances are that they know. Duck, because your cover is blown! With guys, a question is a lot more innocent and straightforward. They're asking a question because they don't already know the answer, but girls ask a question to double-check if their prediction of what your answer will be is correct. Girls ask questions to judge you, but guys ask questions because they have no idea what you'll say.

Gift Bag #7:
Lip Glossary:
Fashion for the DIY Diva

Wearing full-on homemade clothes is tacky (and Amish). But a few choice pieces that look like they came from top boutiques are chic. The trick is to get the right balance between designer and DIY (Do It Yourself). Even if you're not handy with a sewing machine, these DIY tips will have your friends convinced that you're the next Stella McCartney.

I'D LIKE TO TANK THE ACADEMY

Want to add a cool twist to a boring tank? First, find a fun fabric (like an oversize men's shirt at a thrift store). Next, take your tank top and cut it along the seams so that the back separates from the front. Take the back of the tank top and use it as a stencil on the fun fabric, tracing about a half inch extra for a seam. Cut. Now take the front of your tank top inside out and pin it with the fun fabric also inside out. Sew, turn right side out, and now you have a plain tank in front and a surprising design in the back. If you have leftover fabric, you can use it to tie a bow on one of the tank top straps, or make slashes in the front of the tank top and sew the material underneath the slashes.

SEARCH AND DESTROY

Do you want your jeans to look just like those hot boys at the gym: ripped? Here's how to destroy your denim: Insert strips of cardboard into the legs of your jeans so you don't make holes all the way through to the back. Use a cheese grater or sandpaper to tear away at the denim until you reach your desired effect. Cut off the hems and pull gently on the fabric to encourage it to fray. Throw the jeans in the wash and when they come out, they'll be ripped, frayed, and ready to rock.

SIGNATURE SCARF

Silk scarves are like hats—you have some, but you never really wear them. That's about to change, sweetie, because the large, square silk scarf is one of the most versatile items in your closet.

Need a sexy top for a night out dancing with the girls, or a party where you need to make an impression on your crush?

Take a scarf and tie two opposite ends—diagonal from each other—together with as small of a knot as possible. Slip the scarf over your head so the knot is at the back of your neck. Take the two remaining ends— they should be at your hips—and tie them behind your back. If you want to add a twist, literally, twist the scarf once or twice before tying the remaining ends, so it looks like there's a knot at the front of your neck as well.

That's not all you can do with a scarf. If you need a quick purse for running to the mall after school and don't want to squeeze one into your school tote or messenger bag, bring a scarf. Tie the diagonal ends together with some fabric left over, and then place this knot on your shoulder so the rest of the scarf hangs down. Throw in a wallet, cell, and some lip gloss, and then tie the remaining ends together so you have a cool hobo bag. You can turn an Hermès scarf into an Hermès bag without having to pay $4,000 for the famous Birkin.

SHORT BUT SWEET

Want to wear glam shoes (think: kitten heels, platform mary janes) in the summer but don't have an outfit to pair them with? Find a pair of dress pants (a tweed, stripe, or texture works best) and measure a length you'd like them to hit on your leg. Cut three inches below the desired length, fold the extra fabric into a cuff, and sew into place. If you want to go for a rocker look, add metal studs up the sides, or some punk rock pins onto the front hip. Wear with heels, strands of jewelry, and a tank top for an edgy statement that will the other girls in jeans shorts and flip-flops look frumpy.

BAG LADY

Need a bag to take to the gym, beach, or class? Buy a plain tote at a crafts and fabrics store (they're $5 to $10, depending on size) and pick out some cool ribbon to go with it. Hot-glue or sew the ribbon around the top rim of the bag and handles. You can graffiti the bag with a Sharpie or string charms on a chain from one of the straps—or both! If you're computer savvy, buy some iron-on transfer paper and create a design on your computer that you want on your tote. It can be a photo of you and your friends, a pic of Paris or London, or even a designer logo. Follow the iron-on instructions and you'll have a unique tote bag guaranteed to turn heads.

COLOR ME MINE

If you need temporary hair color that will last about a week, either for a party or a night out at a rocking concert, you don't need to buy hair dye. If you have light hair, you can (literally) color it with markers to get precise streaks that aren't stiff with colored gel. Try neon blue and pink for an eighties vibe, or black for a punk look. Be sure to check in with Mom and Dad before you do this, because while it may not be permanent, it still takes some getting used to.

Picture Perfect

Grab an old backpack and make it double as a photo frame. Office supply stores sell clear plastic floppy disc sleeves with adhesive on the back for a couple of dollars. Stick one on the front pocket of your bag and slip in a Polaroid of you and your friends, or a fun magazine collage. Use fabric glue and colorful ribbons to make a chic border and help the disc sleeve to stay in place.

Clique your heels

together and say,

"There's no place like

high school!"

Conclusion
There's No Place Like High School

Even though high school isn't like the opening credits of a teen movie, sometimes it's fun to pretend. With a cheesy pop sound track, no one wearing a visible Abercrombie logo, and clear lines between the populars and the nons, each teen flick makes high school look so easy. But you and I both know it isn't.

Navigating the underworld of backstabbing blogs, hacked MySpace profiles, AIM conversations that got into the wrong hands, wannabe It Girls with serious Napoleon complexes, cute guys who turn out to be horny jerks, extracurriculars that are cool at other schools but dorky at yours, freakish freshmen in your precalc class, urban legends about your lunch line's signature dish, and running into straphangers at the local hangout is the way it really is.

Designer jeans are battle armor, a status bag isn't as hard to snag as a status boyfriend, and a cheerleader doesn't have to win Prom Queen. Welcome to the new world, sweetie, and I hope you're prepared.

It's finally time to step behind the velvet rope of high school popularity. You're on the list, so welcome to the VIP room, darling!

About the Author

Born in 1986, Robyn Schneider is the author of the critically acclaimed teen novel *Better Than Yesterday*. As a high school student, her advice column was a must-read throughout Orange County, California. Now a student at Barnard College of Columbia University, Robyn is a New York City fashionista with a popular blog and a Carrie Bradshaw–like reputation that has reached the pages of *New York* magazine and the *L.A. Times*. Visit her on the Web at www.robynschneider.com.